ABOUT PETE AXTHELM

For a year Pete Axthelm has worked closely with Steve Cauthen, his remarkable Kentucky family and others who know him best in the fascinating world of thoroughbred racing. The result is **THE KID,** an intimate portrait of one of the greatest jockeys and one of the most amazing athletes in history. It is also a broad and highly entertaining look at the horsemen and hustlers, bettors and assorted characters who provide the stage for the feats of The Kid.

Axthelm has been a *Newsweek* columnist for five years, writing on a variety of subjects but concentrating on the world of sports. He has written more than thirty cover stories on topics as diverse as Nadia Comaneci, Secretariat, Billy Carter and "Son of Sam." Axthelm is the author of four other books, including *The City Game,* a highly acclaimed book about basketball.

Now Pete Axthelm has written a marvelous book about his favorite sport—horse racing—and about the most exciting hero to enter the sport in a generation: Steve Cauthen.

THE KID

Pete Axthelm

THE KID
A Bantam Book / June 1978

ISBN 0–553–12000–X

Published simultaneously in the United States and Canada

Bantam Books are published by Bantam Books, Inc. Its trade-
mark, consisting of the words "Bantam Books" and the por-
trayal of a bantam, is registered in the United States Patent
Office and in other countries. Marca Registrada. Bantam
Books, Inc., 666 Fifth Avenue, New York, New York 10019.

PRINTED IN THE UNITED STATES OF AMERICA

To Megan

Introduction

The kid doesn't fit the mold. He strides from the jockeys' room out into the area where the horses are saddled before a race, and some people keep watching for a jaunty angle of the head, a slap of whip against white-clad thigh, or the unmistakable swagger of a little man taking on the world. But none of it happens. Even on horseback, where he does his job better than anyone of his age ever thought of doing, there is no swagger in Steve Cauthen.

He is a hero of our time, a breaker of almost every record in his profession. Yet he seems strangely out of tune with the era. He dominated a season of giants: Reggie Jackson, creating turbulence with his vast shaky ego and then redeeming himself and his paychecks with a few swings of a bat; Bill Walton, who reached down from his seven-foot vantage point and forced an unselfish shape onto the most selfish team sport, basketball; Muhammad Ali, on a final boxing fling, on his own whims, at his own prices. But Cauthen has never sought to match gestures or egos with such men. He still looks out at his world from deep eyes in a beardless face, calling people "Mister" and demanding no accolades.

He is the most honored celebrity in racing history, the first ever to win three Eclipse Awards— thoroughbred Oscars—in one year. He is the winner of more purses in one season than anyone who ever rode horses. He is the Sportsman of the Year. But there is only one honor, one term of identification, that he grasps above all others. He wants to be Steve Cauthen. Unchanged and unaffected even as he rides the dream that he has made real. The kid.

At about the time that the 16-year-old Cauthen was first attracting attention at minor-league tracks in the Midwest, the 14-year-old Romanian gymnast Nadia Comaneci dazzled the world at the Montreal Olympics. Nadia's performance raised an intriguing question. How does it feel to be 14 and perfect at what you do? Soon afterward, Cauthen inspired similar musings on innocence and greatness and how they can coexist. And each time such a question arose, the kid had the right answer.

To understand the star, it helps to know his theater. Horse racing is a game of instant gratifications and fleeting illusions. Pop artist Andy Warhol once said that everyone is entitled to 15 minutes in the spotlight; racing sometimes cuts the act to about a minute and 12 seconds. You win or lose, and then it is time to look ahead to the next race or the next star. The pace and pressure cloud the memory and make the past fade quickly. Loyalties are fickle, reputations fragile. But the kid overcame it all.

The Cauthen phenomenon was framed by two other major news events in racing. Early in his career, Steve shared the headlines with Seattle

Slew, the undefeated colt who was to win the Triple Crown. Like Cauthen, Slew performed his wonders amid images of freshness and innocence. His owners were bright new faces. His trainer defied tradition and marched to his own whimsical drum. His jockey vindicated himself in the face of widespread criticism. The Slew story was a heady one. Its cast became known as the Slew Crew.

Then, after the Triple Crown, it all began to unravel. The owners overreached in search of one more purse, and the colt was beaten. The jockey fired his agent. The owners fired the trainer. The faithful groom also decided to quit. The crew was in disarray, the horse idle in his stall. This story is mentioned not to criticize the people involved but to show what the tense racing atmosphere can do. The Slew story ended sadly. The kid's story goes on.

Later Cauthen was pushed briefly aside by scandal. A veterinarian imported two horses from Uruguay, entered the slow horse in a race at Belmont—and allegedly ran the fast one. A ringer: one of the oldest forms of cheating, brought to life right in the supposedly well-policed New York circuit. The caper sent shock waves through the business. Some horseplayers, suspicious by nature, became all the more certain that the game was rigged. Jockeys, who could always expect to be booed when they suffered slumps or lost on favorites, were subjected to new streams of abuse.

The kid knew one slump in the fall of his great season, and he lost on his share of favorites. He heard the boos but he shrugged them off, and in the end he silenced them with bursts of victories. Gradually the ill feelings and scare headlines of the ringer case disappeared. Like the glorious spring of Seattle Slew, the angry fall of the ringer had run its course. Still the kid's story goes on.

The Kid

Its beginnings lie deep in the Cauthen family history, and so they cannot be precisely located. Its ending is nowhere in sight. But the story doesn't require such boundaries. The Cauthen phenomenon is a present-tense experience: an explosion of racetrack noise and color, a demonstration of riding artistry, a celebration of youth and innocence. You don't measure it or count it the way you count victories or trophies. You savor and enjoy it, for as a Kentucky horseman named Jim Sayler said back when it was all just getting started, "Watching this kid may be a once-in-a-lifetime thing."

THE KID

One

"I have faith in this colt. I've been watching all his races, just like I try to watch every horse's races. I found out that I'd be riding him about ten days ago. I worked him six furlongs at Belmont Park the other morning, so I've got a feeling for him. The trainer, Mr. Kay, says that some riders have had trouble getting him to relax. But he feels relaxed to me. He's got speed and I hope I can use it when I want to. Maybe I can control the pace. The favorites are good horses. But if they make any mistakes, I'll be right there to take advantage."

The words came in clipped, direct sentences, almost barren of inflection. They were accompanied by just a flicker of a confident smile. They were the words of an accomplished horseman as well as a jockey. The two professions do not always go together. Some small men make good livings as race riders without ever learning much about the subtle bone angulations or ailments of racehorses. But this was a jockey who had done his homework,

1

not just ten days before a specific race but throughout his young life. He felt serenely prepared for the task ahead of him. Listening, it was difficult to remember that the speaker had been competing in thoroughbred races for just over a year, or that he was minutes away from perhaps the most important race of his career. It was harder still to match the flat, low-keyed, highly experienced words with a young man, Stephen Mark Cauthen of Walton, Kentucky, who was all of 17 years old.

The date was November 5, 1977. The race was the Washington, D.C., International, at one mile and a half over the grass course at Laurel Racecourse in Maryland. The purse was $200,000 and the prize was quite likely to include the turf-racing championship of North America. But Cauthen had already won an even larger purse in Chicago, and he was the regular jockey on a two-year-old named Affirmed, who was on his way to the championship of his division—and eventually, to the Kentucky Derby. Neither the money nor the prestige seemed to faze the kid. In fact, nothing at all seemed to faze the kid. The International did not strike Cauthen as a particularly significant event in the greatest year of racing ever enjoyed by any jockey— aged 17 or 57.

Steve's mount was a three-year-old bay colt named Johnny D. He had won only one stakes race all year, and had been soundly beaten in his most recent attempt against the best turf horses. He was 10–1 in the betting. The favorites in the race were more than the "good horses" Steve had described. One was Exceller, pride of the 600-horse stable of multimillionaire Texan Nelson Bunker Hunt. Exceller was a worthy representative of the world's most powerful racing organization: he had won major races in France and Canada. The other favorite was Majestic Light, owned by Ogden Mills

Phipps. The Phipps family name had long been dominant in American racing, and Majestic Light was the best Phipps horse to come along in years.

Johnny D., on the other hand, belonged to a small-scale owner from upstate New York, Dana S. Bray. Bray had purchased his first horse only a few years earlier, and it had died. When he tried again, Bray selected Johnny D. at the Saratoga yearling sales. The price was a modest $20,000. And some horsemen had immediately told Bray that his large, ungainly colt would never amount to much. Even when the International drew near, Johnny D. was not invited until the last minute. He was an afterthought.

If the setting for the International seemed to drip with elements of a fairy tale, this was only because most good racing stories come in that form. The late Joe Palmer, wittiest and shrewdest of all racing writers, liked to caution turf romantics that for every ugly duckling that grows up to be a swan, there are thousands more that merely grow up to be ugly ducks. But the swans are what keep racing people hoping and dreaming. And the omnipresent hopes and dreams elevate this vast and often misunderstood sport above the level of a vast numbers game or roulette wheel. "It's hard to die on the racetrack," says an octogenarian handicapper from Florida, "because you're always trying to hang around for the good thing that runs tomorrow." Or for the cheap horse that becomes a champ. Or the teenaged jockey who becomes a once-in-a-lifetime phenomenon. Such dreams are the soul of the sport, and they provide the richest of backdrops for its heroes—the four-legged, 1000-pound variety as well as the baby-faced, 95-pound kid who now stands atop the game.

Years before Steve Cauthen began the long childhood lessons that would point him toward his place in racing's dreams, one brash bettor displayed a painful lack of understanding of all this joyous unpredictability. The man chose a horse that he thought was a sure thing. At the ridiculous odds of 1–10, he bet $5000. For his investment, he stood to win only $500. "That's all right," he said. "What bank pays you ten percent on your money in less than two minutes?"

After the horse had finished fourth and the $5000 bet was lost, another horseplayer asked innocently: "What bank makes you run around the block before you can collect?"

The message endures. There are no sure things. Price tags and pedigrees and predictions all become very unimportant every time a field springs past the steel doors of the starting gate and begins another "run around the block." Racing can be a wonderful leveler. So can a rider like Steve Cauthen.

"We'll be breaking out of the gate right into the first turn," Steve told trainer Mike Kay in the crowded Laurel paddock. *"I'd like to use his speed early to get good position. I don't want trouble on that turn."*

"But you'll have to be careful with him," said Kay. *"Ask him for too much speed and he may get rank with you. Then you might not to able to relax him again. So don't rush him too much, OK?"*

"Yes, sir." Steve was standing still, his five-foot, one-inch frame erect, his whip dangling from his large right hand. International Day is one of racing's celebrity events, and the paddock and clubhouse were teeming with congressmen, ambassadors, and leading turf personalities from around the world. The kid hardly noticed. He was attentive, serious, ready. His brown eyes were fixed on the man he called *"Mr. Kay."* A paddock judge

called out, "Riders up!" Trainer and jockey walked to their colt. Kay formed a cup with his hands, took Cauthen's left boot and hoisted him upward, onto the broad back of Johnny D.

Like Cauthen and thousands of other kids, Mike Kay had once had a race-riding dream. He had attended a Pennsylvania school that provided students with experience around horses and other farm animals. Then he had gone to work for Preston Burch, the man who had literally written the book about training thoroughbreds; Burch's *Training Thoroughbred Horses* is still read by most aspiring horsemen. Later Kay was employed by Preston's son Elliott Burch, also a brilliant and meticulous trainer. Personable and hard-working, Kay had listened hard and learned well.

Once, in 1958, Kay's riding dream had flickered into life. He had won his first race on no less a mount than Sword Dancer, who went on to be a horse of the year. But Kay's jockey career had not gone in the same direction, and he had settled into his role as Elliott Burch's valued assistant trainer. It was not until 1977, when Burch retired temporarily from training, that Kay ventured out on his own. At the time of the International, which showcased some of the most accomplished trainers in the world, 41-year-old Mike Kay was still a rookie.

When Kay decided that he wanted Cauthen aboard Johnny D., he approached Steve's agent, Lenny Goodman. From his big dollar cigar to the tips of his Gucci shoes, Goodman is as cunning and worldly as Cauthen is innocent. In all his business dealings, Lenny is the consummate horseplayer: a seeker of edges and a player of odds. He does no favors for anyone—except the rider who employs him and pays him 25 percent of the money earned.

As he listened to Kay, Goodman had leafed quickly through his mental file. He knew that on the same day as the International, he could have placed Steve on a favorite in a $100,000 race in California. He also could have taken a good mount in a $75,000 race for fillies and mares at his home base in New York. On paper, both of those races had seemed more likely to bring a big victory to Cauthen. But when Kay said that Steve's strong, sensitive hands might be just the right instruments to make Johnny D. relax and run a big race, Goodman had agreed. Goodman, the gambler, had taken a chance. He put Cauthen on Johnny D.

He also placed the kid in very select company. Only a year earlier, Steve had been leading rider at River Downs in Cincinnati, a minor-league circuit where jockeys survived on toughness as much as talent; a local sensation, he had remained untested against top competition. That winter he moved up to New York and performed just as marvelously. But cynics pointed out that many superior jockeys had not chosen to brave a particularly fierce winter and test the kid. Then the summer had brought back the very best—and Steve whipped them too. But the International presented yet another level of competition.

This was a race that belonged to the masters. Eddie Arcaro, perhaps the greatest of all time, had won it more than two decades before. Manuel Ycaza, as fiery and strong as any rider who ever lived, had captured it three times. European winners had included the French champion Yves Saint-Martin and the moody, unorthodox English star Lester Piggott, hero of countless European classics. Most recently, Canadian Sandy Hawley, leading North American race winner of 1976, had won two Internationals in a row aboard Bunker Hunt's horses.

The 1977 field included Saint-Martin on the French distance runner Crow and Hawley on Majestic Light. Exceller was ridden by the ebullient Puerto Rican Angel Cordero, Jr., Cauthen's main New York rival, who had set a record the year before by winning more than $4.7 million in purses. Such credentials might have awed some teenagers. But this teenager was already an established rival of Cordero on the racetrack and a joking friend in the jockeys' room. He had also required only ten months of the year to surpass Angel's earnings record—and he was well on his way to becoming what the headline writers would conveniently label "racing's first $6 million man." Steve Cauthen had long since proved that perched lightly about a small saddle with a set of reins in his wondrous hands, he knew no awe.

"Johnny D. broke from the gate all right, and in the first few yards I could feel that he was handling the track just fine," Steve said later. "But I took a good hold on him going into the turn. Majestic Light's people had said that they might send him to the lead, and I wanted to wait and see what they would do. Whatever way it shook out, I figured I had the speed to use whenever I needed it."

Thoroughbred horse races come in many shapes, with many subplots. Some are predictable, others as unforeseen as a sudden collision or as uncontrollable as a high-strung racehorse's moods. Good riders win the races that go according to well-laid plans. Great riders win the ones that defy logic and demand split-second adjustments and reactions. The International was that kind of race. Cauthen was that kind of rider.

As the eight-horse field settled into the run around the first turn, jockey Hawley eased Majestic

Light into fourth place, then began allowing him to drop back, saving his best efforts for later. Cordero let Exceller drop even farther behind. And Hawley and Cordero began a stalking, waiting game, watching one another carefully to prevent either from grabbing a crucial edge. As the others lingered in the rear and Cauthen placed his mount in the middle of the pack, the early leader—to the astonishment of everyone including his jockey Saint-Martin—was the usually plodding French horse Crow.

Within moments, Cauthen sensed his opportunity and seized it. Almost effortlessly, he surged toward the lead. Soon he was alongside Crow. More important, he was a good eight lengths ahead of his main rivals. Better yet, he achieved his position while moving Johnny D. at a pace that was only slightly above a canter. Even in much cheaper races, a half mile in 50 seconds is considered a slow pace. In the International, the finest turf horses in the world toured the first half mile in 55 3/5 seconds. As the teletimer on the infield tote board flashed the time in lights, trackside observers blinked in disbelief.

"Wasn't the clock wrong?" another jockey later asked Cauthen.

"Nope," Steve said with a grin. "We walked out of the gate and we just kept walking. And that was fine with me. I didn't have to use my horse at all."

For almost a full circuit of Laurel's one-mile oval, Steve remained almost motionless, his body thrust forward, perfectly balanced over his mount's withers. His hands were alongside the horse's neck, calm and still, transmitting his all-important message through the reins to the bit in Johnny D.'s mouth: "Relax." Beneath him, the colt understood.

Johnny D. ran with long, easy strides. He wasted no extra energy by straining for more speed or fighting against his rider. They were a team. And beyond all the technical fine points, that teamwork between man and horse is what superior race riding is all about.

With a little more than a half mile remaining in the race, Cauthen took charge. Instead of waiting for the topsy-turvy, slow-paced race to unfold around him, Steve decided to stamp it with a shape of his own. Inch by inch, he lowered his slim frame over Johnny D. and moved the reins forward to ask for speed. The gesture was so smooth and subtly tuned to the movements of the horse that it was scarcely perceptible to the crowd. But Johnny D. noticed. Suddenly he sprinted away from Crow and opened up a clear lead. First three lengths, then six, then eight.

Far behind, Exceller was floundering and Cordero knew that it was not to be his day. Aboard Majestic Light, Hawley finally stopped worrying about Exceller and took up the chase of Johnny D. But as they turned into the stretch, Cauthen was still nursing a fresh and eager horse—and a five-length lead. With his bold move on the turn, the kid had performed one of the most respected tricks of his profession. He had stolen the race.

Cauthen drove his mount coolly through the stretch. He whipped him several times, then urged him with his hands, then whipped again. Through it all, the movement of his arms never interfered with the flow of horse and rider toward the finish line. "You could serve drinks on the kid's back at the eighth pole," a New York track regular once said. "And you wouldn't spill a drop before he hits the wire." The image was only slightly hyperbolic. As usual, Steve's back remained parallel to the ground. His head was low and icily still. There was

9

economy in every motion. Johnny D. won by two and a half lengths.

The kid rode more than 2000 races in his $6 million year, and he won almost 500 of them. But to those who watched most of those victories, the International stood out. It was not only one of his most important triumphs, but one of his very best rides.

The history of the event only underscored Cauthen's feat. Veterans of the Laurel scene recalled the masterpiece of Saint-Martin back in 1962, when he stalked the five-time Horse of the Year Kelso and finally outfinished him aboard the French challenger Match II. They recalled Piggott, apparently hopelessly blocked, slashing between horses to win in 1968 with the Irish champ Sir Ivor. In fact, astute handicappers had long characterized the International as a peculiarly tactical race: with so many unknown horses from around the world competing under unfamiliar conditions, it was won as often by human maneuvers as by sheer horsepower. "This has always been a jockeys' race," said one Maryland horseman. "And no jockey ever proved it better than this kid did."

In a memorable interlude of two minutes and 32 seconds, Cauthen had displayed brains and skill and rapport with a potentially nervous horse. In racetrack language, he had answered all the questions that a great race could pose. So the postrace interviews seemed almost superfluous.

"This is a real nice colt," Steve began modestly. "Mr. Kay had him ready to run a big race, and he went easily for me all the way."

"Did you have instructions to open up when you did?"

"No, it was my own decision. There were strong finishers behind me, and I thought I could build up a big margin and then hold them all off."

He allowed himself a smile. "It turned out the right way."

Finally there was the inevitable racetrack question, the one that has become a cliché to be scoffed at by knowledgeable riders. "When did you know you had it won?"

Steve didn't laugh. "At the half-mile pole," he said flatly. Then he was gone, to shower and change, to accept congratulations and to start thinking about the next horse he would ride, in some lesser race back in New York. That horse would receive the same attention and preparation that he had given Johnny D. So while others were reaching for superlatives, Steve was already putting his glorious victory behind him. Only weeks later, in a casual conversation in the jockeys' room at Aqueduct, did he drop a hint that beneath his unruffled demeanor, he too had sensed the magnitude of that fall afternoon at Laurel.

"When did you really know you had that race won?" needled Steve's fellow jockey Jacinto Vasquez.

"I guess I finally realized it," the kid said with that slow-forming, infectious smile, "about two days after the race."

Two

The man called Doc was sitting on a tan leatherette chair at the rear of the third floor of the Aqueduct clubhouse. His tall frame was hunched forward, his head half hidden in the thick fur collar of his expensive winter coat. His alert dark eyes peered through steel-rimmed glasses at the figures on the yellow legal-sized pad attached to the clipboard in his lap. It was December 3, 1976, a cold gray Friday without stakes races or special events to distinguish it from any other afternoon in the long New York winter season. But it was to be a day that Doc would never forget.

The horses for the second race were walking from the paddock beneath the Aqueduct stands out across the regular racetrack and onto the all-weather inner track that is used during the cold weather. A few pranced smartly, their nostrils blowing clouds of steam into the air. The rest looked as nondescript as their generally undistinguished racing records. But their appearances hardly mattered to Doc. He is not a student of the conformation of thoroughbreds. He is concerned with numbers. He is one of the most accomplished members of an elite corps of horseplayers. He is a chartist.

Steve Cauthen, 16 years old at the time and a regular New York jockey for less than a week, would not have known a chartist from a nuclear physicist. And Doc would probably not have recognized the beardless new kid from Kentucky if he had bumped into him in the track parking lot on his way home. But in the tightly knit world that is the racetrack, even the most diverse lives tend to touch one another sooner or later. Millionaires brush against lowly and desperate gamblers on the betting lines, and the most humble stable hands share the joys of victory—if not all the spoils— with those who own and train the best horses. So it was not surprising that Steve Cauthen was about to touch Doc where the chartist would feel it most. In the wallet.

"If I ever retired with a lot of money and decided to try gambling on horses," says Steve, "I would never try to be a big-timer. I'd just bet enough to test my skill, like I do when I play cards in the jockeys' room." He pauses, savoring the several thousand dollars he has won playing "racehorse rummy" against older foes in the jocks' room. "In fact, I probably wouldn't bother with betting horses at all. I'd go to Vegas and look for a rummy game."

Doc is a big-timer. He bets thousands of dollars every day at the New York tracks. And he wins. This places him among a very small percentage of people in racing. It also makes him an important figure in the story of a teenaged jockey whom he doesn't even know. For among all the tributes that Cauthen has received from horsemen, journalists, and fans, perhaps none defines Steve's impact on the game quite as forcefully as the hard-won opinion of a chartist like Doc.

A chartist, basically, is a person who brings cold, exacting numbers to bear on the inexact science of handicapping. He feels that there are two kinds of money bet on races: the "dumb" money is governed by the hunches of off-track bettors, the followers of handicappers published in newspapers, and the dupes of touts and rumormongers; the "smart" money is the percentage bet by those who truly understand horses as well as odds.

To secure his position among the smart bettors, the chartist approaches races on two levels. First, of course, he must be clever enough to sort out the horses that have chances to win. Second, he seeks an additional edge by maximizing his return on his winning bets. To accomplish this, he concentrates on the two forms of wagering that attract the most "dumb" money. One is the daily double, in which he must pick the winners of both the first and second races. The other is the exacta or perfecta, in which he must select the first two horses, in correct order, across the finish line in a given race. In either case there are many possible two-horse combinations, each bringing a different payoff. The payoffs are flashed on closed-circuit television monitors throughout the track. As the numbers change, the chartist notes them on the pad on his clipboard. Then he tries not only to bet on the best horses, but to bet most heavily on the ones the "dumb" money has overlooked—the sleepers that will bring him the highest profits.

Charting is no fun. It is painstaking and often boring, and it leaves little time for the kibitzing and byplay that is a valued part of the game for many horseplayers. But it has its rewards. And as Steve Cauthen prepared to ride a longshot named Monsi in the second race on this particular winter day, the daily double promised to be rewarding indeed for the man called Doc.

"I stand to win eight thousand with this horse, ten thousand with that one." Doc's low voice was almost a chant. "Seventy-five hundred, nine thousand, sixty-six hundred. Whoever wins this double, I should make a hell of a score. Unless Monsi wins." Doc grimaced. "But if Monsi wins, no good handicapper deserves to make a score."

Doc had already picked the winner of the first half of the double, a 13–1 shot named Rumancoke. Now he was "alive" with every horse in the second race except the forlorn-looking Monsi. A three-year-old, Monsi had started 19 times in his life without visiting the winner's circle. He had been matched against fellow maidens, or nonwinners, and he had tried to beat horses valued at a claiming price as low as $10,000—with uniform lack of success. He had been second three times and third five times, but he seemed to have no desire to force his way to the finish line in front. In horseplayers' terms, he seemed destined to be a "professional maiden," a noncompetitive type that simply "didn't like the sport."

To underline the bleakness of Monsi's prospects, Doc and other handicappers noted that the docile nonwinner was entered this day against hard-hitting horses that had already won races. The claiming level of the race was $15,000, which is 50 percent higher than that of some races Monsi had already failed to win. Monsi was 19–1 in the betting, and Doc figured that the odds should have been even higher. "This isn't the kind of horse I look at and then eliminate from consideration," Doc said. "This is the kind that I don't even bother to glance at twice."

Around him there were nods and murmurs of agreement. As usual, Doc was surrounded by friends and hangers-on, most of whom were known, as he was, by simple racetrack nicknames. A small, temperamental young guy named Puck Puck, who won his nickname with some betting coups on hockey games, stood to make almost as much money on the race as Doc—as long as Monsi didn't win. A fat, disheveled regular known as Mr. Dirt was in the same position. The race also promised smaller rewards to lesser bettors named Normie-O and Joey and even a chronic loser named Barry, whose financial situation had earned him a nickname parodying that of a pop singer—Barry Money-low. The third-floor regulars were awash in confidence as post time approached. Only one small voice was heard to say, "The only thing about Monsi, today he's got that new kid on him."

."Looking at the horse's form," the new kid was to say later, "I honestly couldn't give him too much of a shot in that race. But I'd already had a few winners in New York and I was feeling good. I figured that anything Lenny gave me to ride had some kind of chance, so I just tried to give my best in every race."

Cauthen had won his first race in New York only five days earlier, aboard a lightly regarded filly named Illiterate. She had paid $61.60. The following day he had brought home another winner, Desert Outlaw. The price had been $18.60. In a matter of weeks, such generous payoffs on Cauthen's mounts would be all but obsolete, as a worshipful public would plunge blindly on every horse that he rode. But as he guided Monsi toward the starting gate, Steve was still forging his reputation. "I'm glad I've been able to get some winners right off," he said casually, "because the only way to keep getting good horses to ride is to make people notice me."

Doc had yet to notice, not because of any lack of attention to detail, but simply because he rarely places much stock in jockeys. Like most astute handicappers, he reasons that on a major-league circuit like New York's, most jockeys are good enough to win when they have the best horses. In order to impress someone like Doc, a rider must be so inept that he ruins his mounts' chances—or so brilliant that he wins races that his horses deserve to lose. There are always a handful of bad riders, or "automatic crossouts," in New York. But by the end of 1976 Doc had never seen the reverse of the equation—a rider so good that he could upset the entire balance of a race. A "hot new kid" who could make a loser like Monsi into a winner? Doc snorted at the suggestion.

Doc was watching on a television monitor as the field broke smoothly from the starting gate on the backstretch of the inner track. Two quick sprinters rushed out to battle for the lead, and the solid favorite, Genuine Silver, settled into good position behind them. Cauthen held Monsi near the rear of the pack. If either speed horse held the lead for the full six furlongs, it would be just fine with Doc and his friends; if Genuine Silver overhauled them, it would be even better. A smile played on Doc's lips as the field turned for home. Then Monsi began to gain on the far outside.

"No," shouted Normie-O, "not Monsi!"

"No, it won't be Monsi," said Doc. Then his throat tightened a little. "No, it *can't* be Monsi!"

But it was. Cauthen reached back and hit the nonwinner with a few right-handed slashes of the whip, then switched the stick to his left hand and hit him again. More important, Steve was using the marvelous, almost indescribable brand of communication that was to become his trademark. Somehow a calm and confident message was traveling through his large gloved hands and through the reins to the horse's mouth—and in a sense, right into his heart. The horse who didn't want to win was suddenly showing not only speed but courage. Under Steve Cauthen, Monsi found that he really did like the sport. As *Racing Forms* were slapped against legs in disgust and moans filled a corner of the third floor of the clubhouse, Monsi got up at the wire to win. His backers collected $40.40 for each $2.00 bet. Doc collected nothing.

"Yeah, I remember that race," Steve said months later. In fact, horsemen have often been amazed at Steve's memory for the habits and tendencies of even the least memorable animals among his thousands of mounts. "That horse had never done much before, but he really ran for me that day. I don't think he ever ran like that again, either. But I remember the day he did."

"Remember it? I'll never forget it," Doc still says frequently. "You can talk about the kid's rides on Johnny D. or Affirmed or any other horse, but he'll never do anything as extraordinary as he did with Monsi. I can see it to this day—the kid moving with that way that only he has, so fluid, so relentless, just grinding down whatever's in front of him." He pauses and bestows a compliment as sincere and meaningful as any of the honors that Cauthen has received. "When you're betting against him," says Doc, "the kid is poison. Pure poison."

Eight days after the Monsi race, Cauthen touched the lives of some other leading handicappers in a more positive way. Horse owner and bettor Len Ragozin and a few cohorts have spent several years in taking handicapping a few steps beyond clipboards and charts; the "Ragozin boys" use an elaborate speed-rating system to help them select horses to bet on—and to buy. The technique is controversial. Many veteran horseplayers insist that the wonder of the game lies in the fact that the thoroughbred horse is designed as well as anything in nature to defy those who would coldly program the future. But others pay handsomely for the privilege of sharing Ragozin's files. And at about the time that young Cauthen arrived in New York, the "Ragozin boys" were set to savor one of the sweetest vindications of their method.

That fall, Len Ragozin had claimed a horse called Frampton Delight for $26,500. After the horse ran steadily in some claiming races, he was entered in the $50,000-added Gallant Fox Handicap. Ragozin was aiming high: Frampton Delight had managed only 1 victory in his previous 21 starts. But the grueling mile-and-five-eighths distance of the Gallant Fox—one of the longest races of the year in New York—figured to help the long-winded Ragozin horse. And the handicap conditions required Frampton Delight to carry only 106 pounds.

As it turned out, the light weight provided an extra edge for Ragozin. Most veteran riders cannot "make weights"—including their own weight and that of a light saddle—and other equipment totaling about 4 pounds—much below 112 pounds. So Ragozin and trainer Everett King decided to try the new 95-pound apprentice in town. It was a gamble: apprentices do not receive the benefit of their usual weight allowances in stakes races, so they seldom get opportunities to win stakes. For all the brilliance that Cauthen had shown in Ohio and Illinois and Kentucky, he had never won even a minor stakes event. "You've got a promising little rider there," King cautiously told agent Goodman. "I'll give him a shot."

"The kid may have a better shot than this horse does," said Lenny.

"I know he's cheaper than most of the others," said King. "But he'll like the distance."

Goodman booked Steve on the horse, but he was not enthused. "It will give you some stakes experience," he told the rider. "But to be honest, this is the first horse I've put you on since you got here that I don't give much of a chance to win."

"Mr. King told me to let Frampton Delight wait and then make one run in the stretch," says Steve. "I knew he looked a little outclassed on paper. But when he warmed up, he felt good to me. I figured that he would rate well and handle the long distance. When some of those other horses would be getting tired, I figured that my horse would be ready to roll."

Frampton Delight began to roll as Cauthen steered him into the stretch. "Whatever you do, don't get him blocked," King had warned the kid in his final instructions. Steve followed orders, moving his horse into the clear and allowing him to stride smoothly and without interference as he passed most of the tiring leaders. Finally he had only one horse to catch—the 3–2 favorite Appassionato. A frequent stakes contender but also a confirmed bridesmaid who had never managed to win a big race, Appassionato was a perfect foil for the kid. Whipping in that rhythmic, "grinding" style that was beginning to impress Doc and the Ragozin boys and every other alert handicapper at Aqueduct, Cauthen roused Frampton Delight to win by a head.

The winner's share of the purse, $33,030, was

more than Ragozin had paid for the winner himself. It was also more than a Cauthen mount had yet won in a single race. When Steve returned to the jockeys' room with his first stakes victory, he was greeted by the two leading veterans in New York, Angel Cordero and Jorge Velasquez. "You deserve this award for beating us in the stakes," announced Angel. Then he and Velasquez presented the kid with a mock trophy consisting of a helmet and goggles. The gesture was doubly satisfying to the kid, because veterans seldom respond so warmly to a newcomer who is quietly removing cash from their established bankrolls—and because Cordero and Velasquez were the jockeys that Steve admired most, even when he began to surge past them in the New York riding standings.

Frampton Delight paid $40.80 to bettors who had anticipated the astonishing triumph. But he was to be among the last big long shots for Cauthen. Earlier that afternoon, Steve had ridden the first three winners on the card. The day before, he had also won with his final three mounts. The string of six straight victories had smashed a record that had stood in New York for a quarter of a century. Cauthen's successes were no longer likely to catch any alert bettors by surprise.

"A New York record and my first stakes win," the kid said with a trace of wonderment. *"I couldn't ask for much more than this."*

The kid's impact on the day-to-day, furlong-to-furlong lives of serious horseplayers is just as significant as the fame he eventually won with better horses in richer races. If anything, the betting angle offers the best proof of the magnitude of Steve's achievements. Like Secretariat and Seattle Slew among recent thoroughbred stars, Cauthen has emerged as a source of romance and excitement in a cold business—a media celebrity with an audience far beyond the racetrack gates. But unlike horses that appear only in brief flashes on the track, Steve has exerted a constant force on the game. By his sheer excellence, he has forced thousands of serious observers—people who earn the right to criticize by putting up their money—to alter their entire way of looking at every race in which he competes. He has changed the texture of his sport.

Very few athletes of our generation can claim a similar role. In the mid-sixties another small-town teenager, Bobby Orr of Parry Sound, Ontario, brought his unique skating talents to the Boston Bruins and introduced both an offensive-minded new style and a shifted balance of power to the National Hockey League. In 1969 the bold words and brilliant play of New York Jets' quarterback Joe Namath propelled the American Football League to equal stature with the older NFL. And Muhammad Ali has restructured the rules of conduct and the financial stakes of boxing throughout his career. But these are giants of the modern era, and it is still a source of amazement to recall how quickly a small Kentucky teenager took his place among them.

As dozens of victories followed those of Monsi and Frampton Delight, millions of dollars began flowing in new directions because of Cauthen. "Dumb" money poured in on every horse he rode, and mounts that deserved to be long shots became favorites because of his presence in the saddle. "Smart" bettors often tried to take advantage of the trend by wagering against Steve, hoping to collect inflated payoffs on his rivals. But he rode such an astonishing percentage of winners that he often thwarted the shrewdest of plans; he left many fans wondering just who was smart and who was dumb. From Monsi all the way to Johnny D., he was the great leveler.

Soon he was even a part of the vernacular. Doc named him Poison, but as one anguished bettor after another watched his fluid stretch drives catch their horses at the wire, handicapper Harvey Pack popularized another cry: "We've been Cauthenized again!" In New York and at every track Cauthen visited, the losers' laments mingled with the cheers of the winners, in a sound that racing has heard all too infrequently. It was a chorus for a star.

Three

"It's a great honor to receive these awards from the people in the game that I love so much. I want to thank the press, my agent Lenny Goodman, and everyone else in racing ..."

It was fairly predictable oratory, but it would have sounded eloquent enough for a senior class assembly back in Walton-Verona High School—which is where Steve Cauthen might well have been that night in January 1978, midway through his 17th year. Instead, Steve was beaming out at an audience of 1200 in the ballroom of the Omni International Hotel in Miami. And his appreciative words—as well as his warm and engaging manner —were striking signs of how much the kid had grown.

Only months before, Steve had struggled to cope politely but nervously with the crowds of reporters, well-wishers, and autograph seekers who greeted him at every track he visited. Now he was looking out at the bejeweled elite of racing's establishment, as well as a large corps of eager fans, inquisitive writers, and photographers scrambling for the best pictures of him. The setting was imposing and the trappings might have baffled Steve only a short time earlier in his life. But he displayed no nerves, and he even avoided the cool remote attitude that he sometimes employed to get through difficult public scenes. He was at ease with the upturned faces and the standing microphone in front of him on the stage. The rented tuxedo fit as comfortably as a well-made set of racing silks.

Michael Sandler, the flesh-and-blood publisher of the *Daily Racing Form* that Steve had always studied as if it had been handed down from on high, had just presented the jockey with a trophy topped with a handsome bronze statue of a racehorse. The statue represents Eclipse, the English thoroughbred who is the progenitor of the vast majority of modern racehorses. Resonant with the history of the breed, the Eclipse Awards also have an immediate impact: they are awarded annually to champion horses and people, as chosen by a highly knowledgeable electorate within the sport. To anyone who has ever bred, handled, or merely loved thoroughbreds, an Eclipse Award is a pinnacle, a once-in-a-lifetime kind of honor. That night in Miami, Steve Cauthen won three of them.

"When I started out to become a race rider," Steve said that evening, *"I never dreamed this big."*

The dream had already taken many shapes. Some people thought you could count it, the way you could count out the kid's world's record purse earnings of $6,151,750 in 1977. Others had translated it into a variety of earlier awards. The Associated Press had named Steve as their sportsman of the year. So had the *Sporting News,* a weekly newspaper with coverage that is usually oriented toward team sports to the exclusion of racing. Almost every club or foundation with an annual prize to give out had followed suit. And in perhaps the most meaningful gesture, at least to the general audience outside racing, *Sports Illustrated* magazine had presented him with the prestigious Grecian urn that goes to its Sportsman of the Year.

Unlike some other tabulators of sporting achievements or reporters' votes, the editors of *Sports Illustrated* have a keen sense of sports perspective—and their audience. Their award is not meant to be a measure of money earned, victories scored, or yards gained; the recipients are often chosen less for what they accomplish than for what they represent. Billie Jean King, for example, might have been considered in a number of seasons. But she won in a year that featured particularly dramatic advancement for women in athletics.

In 1977 there were several candidates who seemed worthy as symbols as well as stars. Center Bill Walton led the Portland Trail Blazers to the National Basketball Association championship; the towering leader also helped his team to affirm the value of unselfish team play in a self-centered era. Slugger Reggie Jackson's World Series home runs for the New York Yankees stood in flamboyant counterpoint to Walton's feats, celebrating the joys of the brash individualism that may be the wave of the future in big-money sports. Both of those contenders also enjoyed a subtle edge that could have influenced circulation directors if not editors: basketball and baseball are extremely popular among *Sports Illustrated* readers, while magazine covers featuring racing have always been poor attractions on newsstands.

But in the final meetings on the subject in their 19th-floor offices on Sixth Avenue in New York, the editors looked beyond all the figures and saw the wider theme that had charmed them along with the rest of the national media throughout 1977. So they sent their best writer of profiles, Frank Deford, to Kentucky to trace the tale of the high-school kid who had conquered such a rugged man's world. Steve was the first racing personality to become *SI*'s Sportsman of the Year. The story was fine, the photographs dramatic. And the headline captured the spirit of the award and the kid's year: "When All The World Is Young."

Steve had accepted that trophy as graciously as he had the others. But somehow his dream seemed best suited to a bronze statue of a racehorse called Eclipse. Perhaps it took him back to all the horses, fast or slow, willing or unruly, who had carried him from the barn behind his home in Walton to the stage of the Omni in Miami. The people he cared most about—the racetrackers—had watched him on those horses along the way and voted to certify his dream year, three times over. There were no surprises in his selection as outstanding apprentice jockey and outstanding jockey. But racing people underscored their admiration for him by voting him the Eclipse Award of Merit. That award usually goes to some visionary leader or statesman who has performed important deeds for the sport or the thoroughbred breed. But in 1977 hardly anyone could think of a person who had brought more prestige to racing than Cauthen. The 17-year-old was racing's Man of the Year.

Surveying the three trophies, Steve looked down from the stage toward a nearby table and motioned for his younger brothers, Doug, 14, and

Kerry, 9, walked up on stage and stood alongside Steve, each cradling one of the awards in his hands and smiling up at Steve. Then, as he concluded his acceptance speech, Steve displayed a final flourish of the sincerity he always had and the sense of timing that he had acquired during his brief career in the spotlight. For a moment he paused, looking down at the ringside table where his parents sat with a few close friends. Then he spoke again, and there was a hint of emotion unlike any that trainers in paddocks or reporters at press conferences had yet heard.

"Most of all," Steve said, *"I want to thank my mother and father, because they're the ones who've done the most for me. And they're the ones I love the most."*

Myra Cauthen, a blond woman with inquisitive eyes and a quick smile, projects a special country brand of beauty and strength even when she is wearing work clothes around the farm. In her rose-printed gown at the Eclipse dinner, she was radiant. And anyone who watched as she listened to Steve, cheered him, and then danced with him could sense a warmth that went much deeper than parental pride in a successful son. Tex Cauthen, with his callused blacksmith's hands and the bad back he earned with too many hard hours on too many unyielding acres, appeared to fit a bit less comfortably into formal wear than did his wife and son. Tex might have savored the moment a little more fully in a flannel shirt and jeans, with a beer in his hand back in his cozy Walton living room. But his habitual wry grin kept breaking into a broad smile as people spoke to him about Steve. In the subtle unspoken way that sometimes eludes

all but his closest friends, Tex too displayed a bond
with Steve that had been forged long before the
first dollar was banked—and will last after the last
one is spent.

Myra and Tex Cauthen, much as they prefer
to shy away from praise and publicity, cannot be
bystanders in this story. The dream that Steve
brought alive at Belmont and Laurel and Santa
Anita was once carried and nurtured by his parents
through hard times and bush tracks from Oklahoma to Ohio to Maine. Even when poverty and
disappointment threatened to snuff out the dream,
Myra and Tex never quite lost the hope that they
could find modest fortune—and vast satisfaction
—somewhere amid the fragile angulations and
mysterious moods of racehorses. So when their first-
born son showed an early fascination with horses,
it was natural that they encourage him.

And that is perhaps the most important word
of all in describing the phenomenon of the kid:
"natural." Myra and Tex never did believe in forc-
ing their own hopes onto Steve or rushing him
past the ordinary routines and rituals of growing
up. They merely allowed a love of horses and a
sense of excitement about them to grow among a
lot of other forms of love and laughter on the 40-
acre farm at 167 South Main Street in Walton.
Even when Steve was very young, Myra recalls,
"He always impressed us with the good head on
his shoulders. He wanted to be in on our thoughts
and decisions." So he was invited into family talks,
and he began to seize the ideas and values that
had been developed long before his birth. Alter-
nately delighted and wary, Myra and Tex watched
Steve's precocious progress around both horses and
people. And as they advised and helped and
warned against too much too soon, a boyhood am-

bition became a teenaged career, and the career
became a dream. It happened the only way the
Cauthens would have wanted it. Naturally.

To understand the special richness of Steve's
background, it helps to define the word "jockey."
On the one hand, admirers of the art of race riding
can claim that the jockey is, pound for pound, the
finest of all athletes. He must have the strength and
guile to control an animal ten times his weight and
the courage to face possible bone-crushing catastrophe every time he breaks from the starting gate.
He needs a keen sense of timing, split-second reflexes, and an ability to communicate with his
mount. Some of these traits are taken for granted
by screaming bettors at trackside, but they will
never be taken for granted by anyone who has
ridden a headstrong thoroughbred. The task demands formidable skills, and the race rider is a
formidable little man.

On the other hand, there is a school of observers that belittles the ability of modern jockeys.
Buddy Jacobson, the leading trainer in North
America in the mid-1960s, was a vocal leader of
this school. "A jockey has less than a ten percent
effect on what happens to a horse in a race," Buddy often said. "His job is to steer the horse and
follow instructions, and so there shouldn't be much
difference between the top twenty or thirty riders
on a given horse. If riding is so complicated, how
come some of our best riders didn't even learn to
get up on a horse until they were about sixteen
years old? Can anyone imagine a baseball player
picking up a bat for the first time at sixteen and
learning to hit a curve ball in time to star in the
big leagues?" To bolster his case, Jacobson could
point to several stars of the 1960s, including Bill
Hartack and Walter Blum, who began riding only

a few years before they emerged as leading jockeys.

Others quibble about riders as athletes from different points of view. Purists from horse shows and jumping competitions point to the unusual "seat" of the race rider on a horse—legs crunched high under him, boots in high stirrups, body perched precariously forward above the horse's withers and neck—and claim that modern jockeys never have to develop the leg control that provides complete rapport and command. They also sneer at the fact that most horses today are sent to the starting gate alongside ponies, because trainers hesitate to trust the jockeys to warm up their horses to specifications and arrive at the gate in good order.

The negative arguments are all too easily overstated, and they take on a very hollow ring when one watches a jockey drive a mount through a treacherous hole between horses, drop a mount's nose down at the precise moment that ensures a photo-finish victory—or crash sickeningly to the ground after a spill. But the critics do bring out an inescapable fact: while jockeys are athletes, they are often incomplete ones.

Some riders, for example, are hungry and brave enough to overcome technical flaws in the way they sit on a horse or handle the whip. Others use cunning to outsmart stronger or smoother rivals. Still others perform wonders from starting gate to finish line, only to prove sadly lacking when they dismount—failing to understand either all-around horsemanship or dealing with people. From the "Handy Guy" Earl Sande of the 1920s through the modern era, there are many heartbreaking examples of top jockeys who ruined themselves with the bold presumption that they could also train horses; then there is Hartack, winner of five Kentucky Derbies, the prime example of a rider who tarnished a great career because he never understood people the way he did horses.

The rare great ones are the riders who take full advantage of their experiences to fill in the gaps in their abilities. Puerto Rican Angel Cordero, Jr., arrived in New York in the mid-1960s with awesome raw talent and finishing power—and gradually directed his exuberant personality away from impulsive mistakes to set the money-winning record that it took Cauthen to break. Panamanians like Jorge Velasquez. Laffit Pincay, Jr., and the recently retired Braulio Baeza are others who got the fullest use out of their skill and courage by adding an element of cool wisdom. Eddie Arcaro and Bill Shoemaker, to mention the two best modern American jockeys, also managed to master all phases of the profession—without ever ceasing the search for some new trick that could win just one more race somewhere along the line. At their best, the great ones are not only jockeys but horsemen and gentlemen. They have it all.

But no one ever had it all at 16. And so in the first months after he burst into the big leagues, Cauthen became the subject of a series of catch-phrases. "You're getting a five-pound apprentice allowance," Lenny Goodman boasted to the trainers who were alert enough to begin using Steve after his arrival in New York. "But you're getting an old rider along with it."

The trainers agreed. "The kid is sixteen going on thirty-five," said one. "Natural ability is one thing. But I've never seen such a case of natural knowledge."

It wasn't natural, of course. It had merely been acquired in a natural way. The Cauthen way. And the manner in which it all began remains as fascinating a part of the kid's story as the triumphs that thousands of fans eventually watched at the tracks. "The only thing better than a lie," the racing aphorist Joe Palmer used to say, "is a true story that no one will believe." In the case of the Cauthen family, the true story is at least as good as the lies and myths that have grown up around the kid. But that doesn't mean that there's anything wrong with the myths.

"You're going to Walton to see the Cauthens?" Lexington horsewoman Anita Madden once joked. "It's easy to find the place. Just drive about seventy miles up the Interstate and look at the sky. There's a star in the East."

Four

"My mom and dad never made me feel like I had to do anything special with my life just to please them," says Steve. "The main thing they taught me was to pick out something that I'd enjoy, and then work hard at whatever it was. I don't think they'd have minded if I'd never made it as a race rider, as long as they knew that I'd given it my best shot. I learned very young that there could be a lot of great times and a lot of hard times in the horse business, and I'd have to work hard in both kinds of times. That's the way mom and dad always did it, I guess."

Ronald Cauthen, who would later be known as Tex, was born in a depression land in a depression year. Dreams were as hard to nourish in 1932 as the crops on his grandfather's hardscrabble farm in Sweetwater, Texas, about 200 miles west of Dallas, and so young Cauthen's ambitions seldom ranged much past the hills just south the farm. Before he was old enough to go to school or meet other kids, he decided that the greatest enjoyment in his life was hunting. At every opportunity, he would pick up his hand-me-down gun and a sack of biscuits and sausage and disappear into the hills that he called mountains. Alone and exhilarated, he would shoot prairie dogs, rattlesnakes, rabbits, buzzards—"I didn't care, whatever moved." He was absorbed into the land and its inhabitants without ever thinking about it. And he learned to ride.

Scuffling across the barren sloping land on horseback, young Cauthen formed some pretty definite ideas about what he didn't like in life. He seldom met other children and didn't particularly care to. He watched his family labor on the 160-acre farm and decided that he certainly didn't like farming. "When I was old enough to have a choice in the matter," he recalls, "I thought for about three seconds about the difference between farming and horses. And I took the horses." At 13, Tex became a horsemen.

You could claim that the brilliance which Steve Cauthen eventually brought to the racetrack had been in the family bloodlines for generations, and you would have a case. Through vague legends that nobody really had time to record during the hard times, Tex is aware that the family traces to three Cauthens, Confederate soldiers from the Carolinas, who migrated to southwest Texas and carved out a living with some shrewd horse trading. There is a twinkle in Tex's eye as he recounts that history, because in places like Texas and Kentucky, there is no more respected roguish art than that of the man who can consistently trade bad horses for good ones. But Cauthen stops short of claiming too many hereditary factors in his own life or Steve's. "A lot of folks in that part of the country come from horse backgrounds," he says. "And even if you descended from the greatest people who ever traded or raised horses, what would it matter? There's probably a lot of priests with brothers in prison. And Bold Ruler may have been the greatest sire that ever lived, but there are a lot of sons of Bold Ruler who couldn't run a lick."

Whatever talents Tex may have inherited were put to a hard and early test. His first employer was an old ranch foreman named Henry Collins, a wizened figure so twisted and beaten by years of riding and falling and getting back up that he could hardly walk on solid ground. But Henry could ride. His specialty was breaking young, half-wild quarterhorses that had never been ridden. He was good at it, and any 13-year-old apprentice who wanted to hang around had to be good at it too.

To teach Tex to break a horse, Henry Collins would tie him into a squeeze gate, a kind of open-ended stall similar to a rodeo bucking chute. When a horse was in place, snorting and bucking furiously for his freedom, the old man would somehow prop young Cauthen onto the horse's churning back. Then he would pull his rope from the bridle and let the horse loose, and Tex would hang on until the animal managed to throw him to the ground. Sometimes he even lasted a few seconds.

If those few seconds gave Collins's squinting eyes some hint that the horse could be handled, he would put Tex back aboard and let him try to last a bit longer. But if a horse seemed too tough for the kid, the old man himself would ride him. Usually, to the bewilderment and embarrassment of Cauthen, Collins would be able to "top the horse out"— or somehow bring him under control. It was a bruising, discouraging way to learn the business, an ordeal that young Steve would eventually be spared. But whenever it crossed Tex's mind that he had been slammed into the hard dusty ground once too often, he thought about life as a farm worker. So he stayed with the horses.

"I guess the closest I came to ending my career in the horse business right then and there was when I had a three-year-old about half broke up on one of those hills," says Tex. "I was just riding him around, doing nothing special, when I saw some deer. I figured I'd teach my horse a little something extra, and have some fun. I was going to maneuver down in front of those deer and try to rope one of them. But the saddle wasn't quite tight enough. About halfway down the mountain, the saddle slipped all the way up on his neck, and of course he got mad and bucked me off. I got tangled in the reins and he drug me all the way down the hill, over the rocks and all." Tex brightens at that point in the tale. "But fortunately, neither one of us got hurt much. So I got back on him and started over. I was still in the horse business."

Soon afterward, Tex got his introduction to "racing." An uncle had a few racehorses and a cousin rode them, and Tex asked if he couldn't get into the competition. He and his cousin began to stage match races across the pastures, and some of the local cowboys and ranchers heard about them. People would bring their own horses out to the field, and Tex and his cousin would ride them furiously cross-country to settle all arguments—and bets—about who had the fastest horses in the area. Long before he ever saw a real track grandstand, Tex heard the cheers of winners and the curses of losers that would echo a thousandfold through the teenage years of his son.

In a state that the Baptists have kept free to this day from the evils of legal wagering on horseraces, the nearest track for enthusiastic illegal betting was in San Angelo, about 60 miles south of Sweetwater. In his 15th summer, Tex ventured down the road to San Angelo, applied to an old trainer for a job, and took on the label that he has worn proudly ever since: racetracker.

"My folks said that I would starve to death," he recalls. "They said nobody makes a decent living around racehorses. I figured at the time that maybe they were right, and there were many days after that when I figured that they had definitely been right. But I still thought, 'What the hell, I'll go as far as I can go with it.' It was what I wanted to do, so it had to be worth trying."

Understandably, Tex estimated that riding horses—or doing almost anything else with them—would be easier than breaking them for Henry Collins. It was, but not by much. In the fields, Tex had always used a western saddle. On the track he had to adapt to a racing saddle. "Like a lot of kids, I thought I could ride anything," he says. "It came as a shock when I started landing on the ground again. That's the thing about horses. Every time you think you know it all, you find yourself starting to learn all over again."

He learned quickly and thoroughly enough to gain the trust of a local horseman who was getting ready to leave the bush tracks of Texas and challenge the established world of racing. The trainer's staff consisted solely of Tex, who galloped and groomed his horses and did whatever else was needed around their stalls. And the man's weapons in his grand adventure were the kind that have driven horsemen ever since man began to ride—two horses, luck so hard that it could only get better, and a hope.

The hope was based largely on one of the two colts, who had shown the trainer and Tex that "he could run quite a bit." The plan was to go to a regular pari-mutuel track, enter the faster horse, bet on him and make a score when he won. Then the visitors could parlay their good fortune by hinting that the second horse, a slow one, was as good as the winner. They would sell him as soon as they heard a decent offer.

The trainer chose New Orleans as his target. The Fairgrounds was a big-time track with a rich history, big crowds, and vast potential rewards. For Tex, at 16, it was a towering setting for a dream. He left Texas and was on his way. He could only imagine how far he would go.

The Texans' grand design arrived intact in New Orleans, and it endured for a soaring five-eighths of a mile around the Fairgrounds track. The trainer and Tex had their carefully saved money bet, and their fast horse was running right to their expectations. He sprinted away from his field at the start, and with just an eighth of a mile remaining in the three-quarter-mile race, he was four lengths in front and accelerating. Standing near the rail alongside the long stretch, young Tex Cauthen felt himself overcome by the tingling, throat-tightening feeling of triumph that tends to take hold of a racetracker and never let go.

Then, sickeningly, the horse "grabbed himself," as the intricate mechanism of his stride altered just enough to make a hind leg clip the back of a foreleg. He took several bad steps, then continued courageously but haltingly toward the wire. He finished third. When he limped back to the barn, he was dead lame. It turned out that he had shattered a sesamoid, a small bone in the rear of his ankle. The horse was worthless. The bet was lost. And no bidders showed up at the barn to buy the colt's slower stablemate. Disgusted, the trainer headed back to Texas.

"I could go back with him and look for a job, in the horse business or someplace else," recalls Tex. "Or I could stay alone in New Orleans." There was no real decision to make. Tex had seen the Fairgrounds and all it promised. He had been part of a scheme, however modest and star-crossed, that had quickened his heart. And he had known that special tingling feeling along the rail, the one that somehow defies comparison to any other sensation in life and thus keeps all racetrackers coming back in search of more. Tex stayed in New Orleans. He was in the horse business.

The question was as inevitable as the usual openers about Steve's weight and height and how he liked being wherever he happened to be that afternoon. At every racetrack that Steve Cauthen visited during his initial tour of the country, there was a welcoming press conference. And at each conference came the cajoling, probing query from some feature writers: "Hey Steve, what do you do for fun?"

Sometimes Steve allowed himself a long-suffering expression as he replied. At other moments he let a smile play on his mouth. He knew that the reporters hoped to hear about hobbies or girls or teenaged pranks. But even after he had discovered attractive females among the autograph hunters of Saratoga or Santa Anita, even when he had shared in jockeys'-room pranks or happy meetings with entertainment and sports celebrities, Steve knew that there was only one honest answer. "My fun is being around horses," he would say. "I've felt that way as long as I can remember. My fun is riding."

"I've had days when it wasn't fun," says Tex Cauthen. "I know Steve has days when it isn't fun. But around horses, I think you reach a point where even the hardest of times can't make you question what you're doing with your life. In my mind, ever since that first trip to New Orleans, I've been doing more or less what I wanted to do. I think Steve developed that feeling at a much earlier stage in his life. For people who work all their lives at something they don't enjoy—something they certainly couldn't say that they loved—it may be hard to understand. But in our family, it's always been something that you don't even have to talk about. I guess the corny way to put it is that horses are in our blood."

Tex's first jobs on his own in New Orleans were not much fun. He worked seven-day, 80-hour weeks at menial tasks around the barns. The names of his bosses, like those of the Texas trainer and his horses, have been pushed out of memory by Cauthen's busy mind. But they were all part of a schooling process that taught Tex a lot about horses. Soon he had impressed one owner enough to get a few horses of his own to train.

It was then that the young loner from Texas got a major lesson about people. One day on the racetrack, a headstrong pony ran away with Tex and dragged him on a frightening tour of the track. When he finally pulled the horse to a halt, Tex was livid. He decided to show the pony who was boss. Hollering and cursing, he dug his spurs deep into the phony's flanks and urged him to top speed: he wanted to teach the phony how "running off" could really feel. He drove the horse for three miles, and when he rode back to the barn, the pony was not only subdued and docile, but totally exhausted and quite possibly ruined as a workhorse.

Unfortunately, the owner who had put Tex into the training business had watched the whole episode. He stormed at Cauthen. "You treated that pony wrong," he said. "You probably destroyed him. He didn't need that kind of handling."

"What this pony really needs," retorted Tex, "is killing."

"What you're going to need in about one more minute," said the owner, "is another job." The argument continued and finally Tex, 18 years old and broke as usual, announced that he was quitting the job that he had thought would be his first big break as a horse trainer.

"The man was partly justified," Tex recalls. "I was too green to know that you can't just do whatever you want on the spur of the moment. Until then I'd always figured that all I needed was to get along with horses. It took incidents like that to show me that I'd better get along with people too." Like many of the lessons that Tex Cauthen had to absorb through pain and poverty, it was one that would later come much more easily to Steve.

Five

"Among all the assets that Steve Cauthen brings to a race," says outstanding New York trainer Phil Johnson, "the most remarkable may be the consistency of his approach. No matter how slow or cheap or troublesome a horse may be, Steve acts as if, for at least that moment, the horse is the most important one that he's ever been on. If he's ridden him before, he remembers little idiosyncrasies that other riders forget. If not, he's studied the horse in the Racing Form. That attitude can be awfully gratifying to the owner who's paying the bills on some horse. Steve makes a man feel that he's getting his money's worth. He never acts like a given race is just another ride around in a circle for him."

"There's no such thing as 'just another ride,'" says Steve. "To the people who own or train him, even the worst horse might be the 'champion' of their outfit. To a small guy in racing, even a cheap race may be the one he's always waited for. You *owe it to him to treat the race the same way he does."*

This attitude wasn't instilled by any Dale Carnegie course. As far as Steve or his father can remember, it wasn't even the subject of any particular lectures as the kid was growing up. There was no need to articulate the joy of winning a race—any horse race—because it was a constant presence in the atmosphere of Steve's youth, as palpable as the manure and liniment smells of the stables. No Cauthen needs to be told that a racing dream can come true without a publicized stakes victory at the end of it. Steve could see that message on the faces of the small-time horsemen who helped him develop at Latonia and River Downs, small tracks near Cincinnati, a few miles from Walton. And he could always sense it in his own father, who learned the same thing when he was at about the age that Steve is now.

After he walked away from his unruly pony and his first training job, young Tex Cauthen joined the vast nomadic labor force that keeps racing alive. Underpaid and overworked, some members of that force are merely content to survive from day to day, always mustering just enough "shipping money" to make it to the next meeting where races will be held. Others compensate for their lowly economic state with the joys of watching horses overcome problems, improve, and win—sometimes with the bonus of a successful bet. Still others cling to a greater ambition, even as they walk horses monotonously around a barn or scoop manure from ramshackle stalls.

Tex belonged to the last of these groups. As he wintered at Hot Springs, Arkansas, and then moved north to small tracks like Beulah Park and Hamilton in Ohio, he was willing to exercise horses and accept almost any other task that would pay off the bills that followed him on the journey. But even when a fairly steady income seemed within his reach as a stable hand, he was always ready to stake what little money he had on bigger things. He wanted to own and train horses—even bad horses—because to a youngster at loose on the roads of racing, no horse was so bad that he couldn't carry a dream.

Steven Cauthen was to attend his first Kentucky Derby when he was three years old—the same age as the horses. A big colt from California, Candy Spots, was the favorite for that 1963 race; his main rivals from the East were expected to be the swift No Robbery and the breathtakingly sleek and attractive Never Bend. But the great rider Bill Shoemaker had some trouble with Candy Spots that day, and No Robbery and Never Bend proved slightly lacking in stamina. A long shot named Chateaugay, ridden by Braulio Baeza, the icy Panamanian who was beginning to build his superb reputation in the United States, rushed through the long Churchill Downs stretch to win it.

That result is just a footnote in the Cauthen story, because the toddler Steve absorbed none of the details of that race. But in the next few years, as he began galloping horses across the fields of Walton, Steve did remember the huge Derby Day crowd and the excitement. Rambling, twin-spired Churchill Downs stayed in his mind the way fairy-tale castles assume places in other young minds. For the kid, the Derby was the first tangible symbol of his goals.

For Tex Cauthen, the Fairgrounds served a similar function. And fittingly, the infield at the Fairgrounds holds perhaps the grandest monument of all to the wild improbabilities of racing fortune —the grave of a horse named Black Gold.

Any time a cynic begins to ridicule some of the more romantic notions about thoroughbred racing, one sure way to bring him up short is to recount the saga of Black Gold. It began before 1920 in the land that Tex Cauthen later knew, around the small tracks of Kansas and Oklahoma, where a cheap mare named Useeit was running often and winning her share. Useeit was owned by a part Indian, R. M. Hoots, whose pride in her far surpassed her modest earnings. Useeit raced in claiming races; these are events in which every horse in entered for a designated price—and may be "claimed" and taken home by any other owner willing to put up that price. The rules of claiming are fairly uniform from Aqueduct all the way down to the bush tracks, but either they had escaped the attention of R. M. Hoots—or his affection for Useeit had blinded him to such technicalities. In any event, there was a day when Useeit was claimed. And when the new owner prepared to take the mare to his own farm, R. M. Hoots refused to give up his horse. Track officials had only one recourse. The game old mare was barred from all racing for the rest of her life.

After Hoots died. Useeit remained on the Hoots widow's land. And one night the horse inspired Mrs. Hoots to have a strange dream. When she awoke, the entire sequence remained clear in her mind: the unknown mare Useeit was bred to the majestic stallion Black Toney—and their foal went on to win the Kentucky Derby. The dream was so haunting that Mrs. Hoots dared to put it all down in a letter and send it to Black Toney's owner, the Kentucky entrepreneur Colonel Edward Riley Bradley.

Bradley was a wealthy landowner, an investor in racetracks, and a breeder who dealt in the world's most prestigious thoroughbred bloodlines:

in his career he bred four winners of the Derby. But above all he was a gambler. Once he appeared before a U.S. Senate committee investigating crime and described his occupation as "speculator, race-horse breeder, and gambler."

"What do you gamble in?" snapped Senator Huey Long of Louisiana.

Bradley's voice was quite and proud. "Almost anything," he said. And he was right. He was always ready to take a chance or try an innovation, with his horses or his life. So he was an easy touch for a woman with a wild hunch. He read Mrs. Hoots's letter and gave her a free breeding right to Black Toney. Useeit's foal was named Black Gold. In 1924 the colt won the Kentucky Derby. And for decades afterward, his tale kindled sparks across hundreds of small racetracks where young men like Tex Cauthen worked with horses.

The first horse that Tex owned was not sired by Black Toney or any other remotely fashionable stallion. It was a son of a cavalry remount stud called The Porter. A remount stud is used to supply fresh horses, or remounts, for the military; it would be a fluke, obviously, if such a horse produced an offspring with racing speed. Tex's horse, called Texas Portden, was no fluke. He was every bit as slow as he was bred to be.

"I bought Texas Portden for a thousand dollars, on the cuff," Tex recalls. "There was no cash involved, naturally, because I didn't have any. I was going to pay back the price out of whatever the horse won." There were no winnings. Most horses that are worth keeping "break their maidens" by winning their first race by the time they are four years old. If a horse is still a maiden at five or six, he is often barred from cluttering up the track at any respectable race meeting. Texas Portden was a six-year-old maiden.

"Things didn't look too bright for him," says Tex. "I took him from Hot Springs up to Ohio, and I followed a rough routine. I'd find a place to stay on the cuff. I'd convince whoever ran the track kitchen to feed me on the cuff. Then I'd gallop enough horses for other people to get up the money to pay everybody. And the horse and I would move on."

At River Downs, Tex joined in an unlikely partnership with another struggling one-horse owner. George Dobkin's horse, Master Insco, was a five-year-old maiden. Like Texas Portden, he had never finished anywhere but last in a race; his sire, Master Mark, was every bit as obscure as The Porter. But Master Insco had two distinguishing traits: his massive size and the unbelievable spell he cast over owner Dobkin.

"I've been trying to buy this horse for months," Dobkin told Cauthen. "But even when he finished last four straight times, the owner hesitated to sell. The trainer said he didn't know who was crazier, me for wanting the horse or the owner for not wanting to get rid of him. Anyway, I finally bought him." The price was the familiar currency of the times, $1000 on the cuff. "But I don't think I'd be more thrilled," gushed Dobkin, "if I'd just bought Native Dancer from Alfred Vanderbilt."

Brought together by enthusiasm for their horses, Dobkin and Cauthen decided to join forces. Well aware that their aging maidens would not be entitled to stall space, they sneaked into the River Downs stable area by night and bedded down their charges before the racing secretary could find out. When he did discover the uninvited guests, the secretary fumed for a few minutes and then grudgingly allowed them to stay—if only as a curiosity. "In the history of racing," sputtered the secretary,

"I don't think any one outfit every assembled a pair of worse horses at the same time."

Texas Portden brought no happy endings. Cauthen was happy when he finally managed to give him away—and transfer the "cuff" of his purchase price onto the new owner. But the hulking Master Insco, a 1350-pound beast that Dobkin felt was the biggest if not the swiftest thoroughbred of all time, gradually showed trainer Tex some hints that he could run. In his first race for Cauthen and Dobkin, he was fifth. Then he placed fourth, earning a $35 check that was reason for some wild celebration. After two more good races—a third and a second— Tex figured that he was about to win his first race as a trainer.

"Actually, we had some chances to sell that huge horse for somebody to use as a jumper or hunter," says Tex. "We might have gotten three or four thousand for him, which would have been an intelligent thing to do. But old George was getting some money from some wealthy relatives at the time, and he was afraid that if he did anything that showed a profit, they'd cut him off. And as the weeks went by and the horse improved, I guess you couldn't have pried him away from George."

On the afternoon of Master Insco's biggest race, George Dobkin thought he saw an omen. During the post parade on the very muddy track, the horse seemed to pause as he passed the spot where his owners were leaning on the rail. Tex assumed that Master Insco, a friendly, playful giant around the stable, was merely showing a flash of recognition. Dobkin read more into the moment, and long after the race was over he maintained that the horse had been trying to say, "Goodbye, friends."

Master Insco broke slowly in the 1 1/16-mile

race, and jockey George (Pat) Ryan allowed him to settle into stride in fourth position. On the far turn he was still far back of the leaders, but then he swung to the outside and began to churn through the mud toward the leaders. Tex felt that special sensation he had first known at trackside in New Orleans. As the field passed where Dobkin and Cauthen were standing, Master Insco was second and still gaining. At the wire he thrust his nose in front, and the owners let out a wild whoop. "A cyclone finish, a magnificent performance," Dobkin kept saying as he stood in the winner's circle. Tex stood nearby, smiling and speechless. He had won a horse race.

When all the winner's circle pictures had been taken, Tex began to lead his prized horse toward the paddock, where all winners undergo a saliva test. Master Insco followed for a few long clumsy strides. Then he faltered suddenly, pitched forward, and collapsed at the feet of his owners. He was dead of a burst artery near his heart.

"I've never owned a stakes horse or even a fairly good horse, by most standards," Dobkin was to say for years afterward. "But in a certain way, Master Insco gave me a kind of greatness that no horse could ever top."

Tex Cauthen was slightly more philosophical. "When you win your first race and then your horse drops dead on you," he says, "you've been through the highs and lows of the game about as quickly as anyone. Looking down at that great big dead horse, I knew that I was out of the horse business momentarily. But I also knew what it had felt like watching him win. And so I knew that I'd be back."

The peaks and valleys of the business leveled off somewhat for Tex in the following years. In 1952 he entered the army, where he was trained as a meteorologist and stationed in Panama. "It was a nice easy job for a while," he laughs. "I've always figured that if a person wants to be a bum, the army is a good place to do it, especially at a nice quiet post outside the U.S. The trick is to find a place where nobody wants to go and nothing much is happening. Then you have plenty of time to goof off. And to think."

Some of the thinking led Cauthen to the bittersweet conclusion that he might not be the anointed heir to great trainers like Ben Jones or Sunny Jim Fitzsimmons. Lack of luck and lack of funds had alerted him that his career as a horseman might provide something less than an ironclad annuity. So when he left the army, he set out for a slightly more secure trade: he enrolled in a three-month agricultural-school course in horseshoeing at Michigan State University.

He took to his new profession. But even as he bent to drive nails carefully through aluminum shoes into the hooves of horses, Tex's gaze remained fixed on something higher. The young loner who had started out in Texas had become an infectiously charming character in his few years of racetrack life. George Dobkin was only one of many friends who listened raptly to Tex's grand plans and did everything they could to help make them come true.

While Cauthen was in Panama, for example, one friend scoured the bush tracks in favor of castoffs and cripples from other stables—in the serene belief that Tex could turn the ugly ducks into swans. Tex looked them over, saw the overwhelming challenge they presented—and naturally couldn't resist. The blacksmith course was in East Lansing, Michigan, and the dozen horses were stabled in Carthage, near Cincinnati. But at the time, this seemed only a mild inconvenience. Tex decided that he would commute to Carthage on weekends, train the horses, and then leave instructions on what to do with them while he went back to school.

Some of the finest horsemen in the world have learned that training by long distance is all but impossible. If you can't be there to sense precisely how tired your horse got in a workout or to note some slight heat or inflammation growing in a troublesome ankle, you aren't training; you're hoping. Even to attempt such a long-distance regimen requires vast experience and superb assistants. Tex had neither. So while the blacksmith school was teaching him one phase of racing, his horses were teaching another—while he and his friend paid the tuition bills. "I fooled with those horses through one meeting at Carthage and another at Beulah," he says. "And all I found out was that there wasn't one in the lot worth fooling with." It was the kind of lesson that had to be learned the hard way—but only by one generation of the family. By the time Steve began feeling his own way around the tracks, he seldom approached any task without all the experience and preparation he needed to succeed in it.

Tex turned some of his slow horses over to the man who owned them and made a few others into stable ponies so he could sell them for salvage value. It seemed like time to get down to shoeing some horses and making some money. But for Cauthen, there always seemed to be one more five-year-old maiden to try. The next one was waiting down in New Orleans. Tex bought him and went to work on him. On the cuff.

"The horse was a rogue but I thought he could run," Tex recalls. "One day I thought I'd straightened him out by putting blinkers on him. I took him out to the starting gate to school him one morning, and I was pretty confident that the blinkers would keep his mind on running. Then the starter said that I wasn't allowed to use blinkers in the gate. I said, 'What the hell, I'm here, might as well break him once from the gate without the blinkers.' That was my mistake."

In the simplest terms, the purpose of blinkers on a racehorse is to force him to look at where he is going. Blinkers, affixed to a hood over the horse's head, come in many shapes, from very small flaps to large cups that restrict a horse to very narrow tunnel vision. Sometimes blinkers merely encourage a horse to ignore distractions. In more severe cases, they keep a skittish horse from seeing things that might panic him.

Cauthen's maiden was one of the severe cases. As the steel door of his stall in the starting gate slammed open in front of him, the horse had a splendid view, unhindered by blinkers, of enough horses, people, and objects to stir him to a frothing rage. First he tried to dig his feet into the track, prop suddenly and hurl Tex over his head. Then he tried to wheel in a circle, directly into the flow of oncoming traffic on the track. Tex hit him once on the side of his head, and thought he had him pointed in the right direction. But after they had galloped for an eighth of a mile, Tex anticipated trouble. The horse, he was sure, was getting ready to bolt to the outside. Tex braced himself. Then the horse fooled him and bolted to the inside. Tex fell over the inside rail and broke four bones in his leg.

Like the army, crutches give a man a chance to think. By the time his long cast had been cut down to allow him some mobility, Tex was looking for steady work again. For a while he got back into the pony business. He would buy ponies at sales down in Indiana, train them until he could use them to lead horses to the post at River Downs—

and then sell them as quickly as somebody showed an interest. Business wasn't bad, but as he approached 25 and figured that he had served enough apprenticeship as a blacksmith, Tex decided to begin shoeing horses full-time.

At River Downs and New Orleans Cauthen did some shoeing for a trainer named Tommy Bischoff, who ran a stable owned by his father, a grand character of Ohio and northern Kentucky racing, Ed A. Bischoff. Tommy Bischoff had a good-looking blond sister who "walked hots" or cooled out horses for him during her vacations from school. Tex and the girl had nodded and smiled at one another a few times over the years. But it was one day when Tex was shoeing a horse and Myra Bischoff was holding its head that they first began to talk. Within a year and a half, the blacksmith and the hot-walker were married. And Tex was already thinking of changing those titles. He yearned to be an owner again. And he wanted Myra to become a full-fledged trainer.

"I'm not really a trainer," Myra Cauthen says modestly. "I'm more of a groom with a license."

"That's not true, because Myra won her share of races," says Tex. "We've got the winner's circle pictures to prove it." He glances proudly at his wife. "Yep, when I married this girl I changed her from a hot-walker to a trainer." He laughs. "Boy, was that a dirty trick."

Six

"From the time I started winning races," says Steve Cauthen, "people asked me how I planned to keep from getting the big head. That always surprised me, the way people expected that just because a race rider was doing good, he would get too high on himself and ruin it all. They'd say, 'Look, he's winning all that money and he just acts like a regular kid.' But they don't know our family. The first time one of us ever stopped being regular kids, mom would say something that would put us back in line. Mostly, she'd figure a way to make us laugh at ourselves for being so dumb."

"The thing I loved most of all the stuff written about Steve," Myra Cauthen once told this writer, "was when you said that he better watch out for the temptations of tall women. We all laugh about that image. Steve laughs about it too."

Tex Cauthen's joking aside, life has played few dirty tricks on Myra Bischoff Cauthen. Horses and hard work and a close family have always been part of her life, and she has dealt with all three with a quiet sense of perspective and a sound of soft laughter. "I don't have the gift of gab like Tex does," she says. "Telling stories isn't my style." Her conversational manner runs to one-liners, the kind that keep even the most prodigious kid from "getting the big head."

"When he was growing up, Steve always seemed to have a comeback for every comment," Myra recalled recently. "He didn't talk that much, but what he said got to the point. Some people say that he and I are alike that way." As she was speaking, Doug Cauthen bounded into the living room, brandishing a looseleaf notebook. A Kentucky blizzard had kept the boys home from school that week, and they were due back in class the next morning. "Well, mom," Doug said, "I got all my homework done."

"Wonderful," Myra said dryly. "You only had a week to work on it."

When you have met the parents of other teen-aged sports sensations, it is tempting to compare Myra's style to that of a Gloria Connors, who has pushed young Jimmy so hard and ruthlessly to the top of tennis, or a Colette Evert, a fine low-keyed woman who has helped daughter Chris to remain level-headed and delightful in the face of success —but who has submerged much of herself in the endless arrangement of meals and travel schedules around tennis practices. But such comparisons are unfair, not only to the other women but to Myra Cauthen. This is not merely an extraordinary sports mother. This is an extraordinary mother and woman, and she would be the same if Steve were about to graduate from Walton-Verona High and pursue a career that no one would ever hear about.

Edward A. Bischoff was an old man in a nursing home by the time his grandson Steve began jogging victorious horses into winner's circles. Often Myra would take the pictures of those victory ceremonies to her father, and he would look at them for a long time, smiling and nodding with joy and appreciation and perhaps even a faint feeling that he had suspected something like this all along. Those were bright moments for the old man and warm ones for his daughter. And they will outlive Ed Bischoff by many years in the Cauthen family memories, as one more confirmation of the fact that what Steve is accomplishing began long before the first starting gate burst open in front of him. Generations before.

"We had horses as long as I can remember," says Myra. "I can remember when we were little kids, maybe four or five, being at the old Latonia track with daddy." Ed Bischoff's luck was a contrast to that of young Tex Cauthen: his very first horse, named Orchestration, finished second in his first start at Latonia and paid a startling $600 to place. The price is still a record. And the horse didn't even drop dead after the race. "I don't think daddy ever made a lot of money in racing," says Myra, "but he had a lot of fun and so did we."

The Bischoffs lived in Park Hills, a suburb near Covington, Kentucky. But the kids—Tommy, Myra, Joan, and Nancy—spent weekends and summers at the family farm in Richmond, about five miles from Walton. Like young Tex Cauthen down in Texas, the kids learned to ride and take care of horses at an early age. So it was quite natural years later when young mother Myra propped her first son aboard a painted pony at the age of two and proudly took a snapshot.

Myra and sister Joan were teenagers when they first noticed a part-time blacksmith and trainer who they decided was "cute." Five years passed before Tex Cauthen and Myra got a chance to talk while they worked around the barn, but they quickly found much in common. By the time they married, there was no question about what they would do together. It was just a matter of where. The first stop was Scarborough Downs, a small track near Portland, Maine.

"Myra had got together some horses to train and we got ourselves off to a fine start," says Tex. "We won six or seven races up in Maine and I paid off a few old debts. But we were having such a good time, we didn't pay much attention to the value of the dollar. So by the time we were ready to ship out of there, poverty had struck again."

The couple moved on to Rockingham in New Hampshire, then Chicago. Tex was shoeing horses and Myra was training some, but victories were elusive. The memories of those days are filled with promising little fillies getting shut off in races they should have won, other horses getting carried wide just as they commenced what should have been winning moves—the kind of things that can happen to any jockey, but would never seem to happen to Steve. Then the Cauthens headed for New Orleans, with a little more ammunition than Tex had brought on his first try at the Fairgrounds. They had a filly named Tricycle, and she was the best thing that would happen to them in racing. Until they had a son.

"We run Tricycle the first time down there and she win," Tex says in the present-tense vernacular that racetrackers often employ for their happiest tales. "We run her back, and she win again. Then she run back and she got beat a nose. And we lost her. She was claimed out of the race. But Tricycle had been good to us. She let us get together a few dollars for a change. And that was a good thing. Because when Tricycle was running for us, it was getting to be Steve's time."

Reminiscing about the days that led up to Steve's time, Tex and Myra recently rummaged through an old carton stuffed with photographs. There are pictures of the wedding, of other parties, and of course of winner's circles. "Daddy always seems to be laughing at something," Myra said. "He's always been a real character in any group."

"The best way to describe him," said Tex, "is that he was ready. When we were in New Orleans, if I said let's go drink some beer and eat some oysters, he was ready. If I said let's take a look around Bourbon Street, he was ready. If I said let's go out to the races and see if we can't find something to bet on, he was ready. He's one guy who never had any problem figuring out how to enjoy life."

"Here's a shot of the priest who came all the way from New Orleans to Kentucky to marry us," said Myra.

"I always wondered if he knew something I didn't," said Tex. "Coming all that way, I figured he must have wanted to get us married awful bad." The laughter filled the snug kitchen where they sat at a small table. Then Tex Cauthen fingered a few of the winner's circle photographs, and reflected for a moment on why there weren't more of them.

"Some of my lack of success those early years was due to misfortune," he said. "And a lot of it was poor judgment. A few times, I was close to getting hold of some real nice horses, and then it would fall through because somebody who was supposed to come up with some money didn't come up with it. But basically, my problem was that when I couldn't get the good horses, I went on and grabbed whatever horses I could get. I spent too many mornings with horses that weren't worth the hours. But you know how it is, you always hope you can do just a little better than somebody else did with a horse, or at least get a little luckier than the other guy . . ."

The refrain was as old as the sport itself, a song of hope tempered with a hard-won sense of realism. "If you summed up my career, I guess you'd have to say that as a horse trainer I was unsuccessful. As a horseshoer I have been successful." Tex smiled. "But of course, there are not too many failures as horseshoers."

Another snapshot jogged Tex from his wistful mood. "That one was taken at a rattlesnake hunt," he said. "Back in my hometown, they had one of the biggest annual rattlesnake hunts in the country. Some folks came with poles with fancy clamps on them to grab the snakes. But I had some cousins, including one little girl about nine years old, who could just make a loop of rope on the end of a stick and pick up rattlesnakes with it."

"I've heard *you* talk about hunting snakes," said Myra. "I didn't think a whole town did that sort of thing."

"One day I'll never forget, I shot a rattler in two with a shotgun," continued Tex. "The front end crawled away into the bushes, and I just threw the back end in my pickup truck and went on in to dinner. Later I was out shooting some more, and I found that head end. It had crawled off into the sun and died. So I worked my shotgun up under the snake and balanced it and carried it back to the group. Then I flipped it high in the air and it came down end over end into the middle of all my aunts and cousins, just kind of smiling at them. Funniest thing I ever saw. Just about scared them to death."

"Hilarious," Myra said to a female friend. "Wouldn't you love him?"

But amid the laughter, the answer to that question was inescapable. Love showed in the faded, half-focused snapshots as clearly as it did in the stories about the early days. It was particularly evident in the last of the victory pictures of the time, the ones featuring not only the game mare Tricycle but also one of the few trainers in history to win races while she was very pregnant. "Those were about the last of my serious training days," Myra said. "Later on, I concentrated more on the kids."

It was getting to be Steve's time.

Seven

"When Steve was a little kid," said trainer Teddy Cleveland to some friends in Florida one winter, "he was the meanest little kid in Kentucky, maybe in the whole Southeast. Any time you saw him coming, you had two choices. Either bolt everything down, or get out of the way." Cleveland, who used to be married to Myra Cauthen's sister Joan, seemed in a position to know such things, and when he made his comment it was widely circulated. But other witnesses tend to disagree.

"Ted made that remark at the time when Steve was doing so well and everybody was saying nice things," says Myra. "Maybe he just wanted to be different and stir up some attention. Steve wasn't a bad kid. He was just full of energy."

"I don't remember being all that bad," says Steve. "And if I was bad, I suspect my parents would have done something to make me remember it. What I probably was," he adds, borrowing an expression used mainly to describe nervous young *thoroughbreds, "was sort of 'on the muscle' all the time."*

Myra Cauthen journeyed back home to Covington to have her baby. Steve was born on May 1, 1960. He weighed seven pounds, 12 ounces—a normal weight giving no hint that he would grow up small enough to be a jockey. His parents certainly had no thoughts in that direction. They were delighted just to have a healthy, noisy addition to the family.

The Cauthens took the new baby back to New Orleans, where they were racing. They lived in a house trailer for the first year, but one day they found that Steve had crawled out to the edge of the Airline Highway nearby. "We got to get out of here," said Tex, "before the kid gets himself killed." They switched to an apartment, then a house. Then Myra came into a little money and they decided to buy a farm in Oklahoma.

It was there that the year-old Steve was hoisted aboard his first horse; he actually began to ride ponies when he was two. "Folks are making a lot of that now," says Tex. "But where I came from, it wasn't all that unusual. Just about every kid got on a horse as soon as he or she could in Texas and Oklahoma. I had a cousin once who could ride a pony bareback on the dead run when she was five."

Steve was to develop even faster than that, but his prowess did nothing to alter Tex Cauthen's nagging bad luck. The Oklahoma farm failed. "We bought some cows, Santa Gertrudis, and hoped to breed them," says Tex. "We also had a thoroughbred stallion called Protocol and we hoped to get some mares bred to him. But we were too far from most racing people, and Protocol wasn't exactly the kind of stallion that you'd ship a mare across country to breed to. We tried hard to keep things going out there, but the farm just wouldn't work for us. Finally we had to fold it up."

For a while the Cauthens lived back in New Orleans. Then they looked for a place in the fast-growing Florida horse country near Ocala. Finally a friend told them about a nice spread up in Walton. It was convenient to the Cincinnati area tracks where Tex could do some shoeing. And even if it was light-years from the rich land 70 miles south in Lexington, it was the kind of Kentucky land where, if a man got lucky and put some cash and some good mares together, he could raise a horse. The Cauthens bought the Walton farm in 1965. Their second son Doug was born at about the same time. They were ready to settle down.

The road from the Interstate into Walton runs straight for a few miles, then narrows over an old railroad bridge. At the corner where it meets Main Street—the main artery that includes the three-block business district of the town—there is a sign identifying the Walton Church of God: "Jesus Saves, Jesus Heals." In good weather a few old men can be found passing the time of day outside the drugstore, some even grumbling that the town's young hero may turn Walton into a tourist haven, "like Plains, Georgia." Customers in the beer joint and the two gas stations can also be heard discussing crops and the weather and sports, as rural people do in thousands of similar small towns. But contrary to the images held by some of the Cauthen mythmakers, Walton is not a poor backwoods town. There are a few fine homes owned by wealthy people, and a number of middle-class households belonging to refugees from Cincinnati.

Once Walton was undoubtedly a kind of frontier, populated by hardy folk willing to engage in constant battle against soil and weather conditions that were less than ideal. In the future it may well be subdivided and organized into a full-fledged suburb, with shopping malls and ranch houses like the ones up the Interstate in Florence. But now, in the time of Steve Cauthen, it rests between those poles. It is a town without a dominating theme, a suitable place for a modest 40-acre farm. A nice place in which to grow up innocent.

"You're lucky you're a hillbilly," veteran Panamanian jockey Jacinto Vasquez once teased Steve. "You only had to think about riding, while the rest of us had to resist all the broads and thieves and pimps."
"What's a pimp?" asked the kid. "Is that a guy who sells dope or something?"

The Cauthen farm lies at the southern tip of Main Street, just before another railroad bridge that leads out of town. It is several hundred yards south of the last of the commercial buildings, Travis's Gulf service station. When Steve and Doug were little, the family had a rule that the boys could not wander alone past the station. Nine-year-old Kerry is now bound by the same regulation. But the boys have never felt particularly restricted, because much of their recreation is not up the road but out behind the neat, plain wooden farmhouse. There the Cauthens have always maintained a handful of horses and some other animals. When the kids aren't riding, there are plenty of other chores to occupy them in the barn and across the pastures.

Walton is a town that still knows the clatter of fast-moving trains. One of the two tracks in town runs along the eastern edge of the Cauthen property, and when the Southern freight chugs past, the engineer happens to blow his whistle at the bridge just past the house. The sound is loud and shrill and it lingers when the train has gone. It is the kind of noise that has inspired countless country songs about small-town kids with a lust for wandering. But Steve doesn't recall being particularly inspired by it. He was in no rush to wander, at least until he had built a firm foundation under his ambitions. And when he did think about moving on, the transportation he envisioned always had four legs.

The railroad does have one connection to the farm; the Cauthen fence posts are huge wooden slabs that once rested under the tracks. Railroad workers had discarded them during some repair work before the Cauthens arrived; they had left them near the bridge, down a gentle hill from the farm. Tex Cauthen is a compact man, about five feet, nine inches tall; his only obvious sign of strength is his powerful blacksmith's forearms. But when he began fixing up his farm, he somehow picked up those hulking railroad ties, dragged them up the hill, and drove them into the hard ground for his fencing.

"Most racetrackers figure that I got this bad back bending over the horses that I shod," says Tex. "I believe I got it right here on the farm. It was the same as it was with the horses—I thought I could do just a little more than I should have. This bad back comes from trying to fix the place up and pay off the mortgage in too much of a hurry."

"Whatever they did to his back, those railroad ties tell me a lot about Tex and his whole family," says his close friend, trainer Lonnie Abshire. "There's a lot more strength there than you can see with your eyes."

Steve was five when his weight began to level off at about 35 pounds. As he and his parents noticed that he was somewhat smaller than other kids, they might well have nursed their first thoughts about his future in racing. It would have made a good episode in the "Star Is Born" myth. But it didn't happen. Until he was 12, Steve never spoke of any ambition to ride in races. The joy of galloping across a pasture was more than enough —for the kid and his parents. Only a few friends of the Cauthens began to suspect that something special was going on in those fields.

Frank Tours is a racing official whose career has taken him from Latonia to the big California tracks and New York; he is now director of publicity at Hialeah in Florida, and his skill is such that he is gradually convincing the racing world that there is vitality in the beautiful Florida track that had been given up for dead. Tours is a lover of horses and horsepeople, but like many who have spent their lives in that pursuit, he is also cautious with his affection. He has watched Swaps and Secretariat and Seattle Slew and he has given them his warmest approval—but only after it was earned. He treats riders the same way, and so his opinion is among the most respected in the business.

"I was working at Latonia in 1965 when somebody told me to come out to Walton and look at something unbelievable," Tours recalls. "I was skeptical, but I went. And I saw this tiny kid handling a thoroughbred in a full gallop, sitting over him like a regular exercise rider. I never forgot the name Steve Cauthen after that. You don't forget a kid five years old who looks that good on a horse."

Tex Cauthen built up a good business in those first years in Kentucky, shoeing horses on the nearby tracks and several farms. Long ago, the blacksmith was one of the noblest artisans of rural America, standing patiently over his fire and anvil to shape steel shoes to the needs and idiosyncrasies of a community's horses. Then the automobile nudged him out of the mainstream of commerce and he was relegated to the farms and other areas where horses were still essential. More recently, the advent of the aluminum horseshoe has simplified the trade, allowing the smith to substitute some rudimentary bending and fitting for the painstaking heating and hammering of the old steel era. Standardbred horses—pacers and especially trotters—still require subtle adjustments in shoe styles and weights, and so the blacksmith retains much of his old honor in harness racing circles. But some thoroughbred horsemen now consider shoeing a fairly basic affair, requiring hard labor and diligence but relatively little imagination or horsemanship.

Only a few horsemen have continued to hold shoeing in the highest esteem. But those horsemen also happen to be among the best. "No foot, no horse," intoned John E. Madden, the "Wizard of the Turf" who bred five Derby winners at the turn of the century. Wise trainers listened to the words, and leading modern horsemen like Allen Jerkens and the late Eddie Neloy have been renowned for choosing their blacksmiths well and supervising them carefully. The late Hirsch Jacobs, probably the greatest of all modern trainers, never considered shoeing a routine task to be left to someone to do after training hours; he could be found every morning, long after others had departed the stable area, standing over his blacksmiths and comparing notes with them in his chirping singsong voice. Naturally these meticulous men demanded blacksmiths who cared as much as they did about horses. And so even in the mass-production aluminum era, an elite band of old-fashioned, thorough blacksmiths has endured around most tracks. At places like Latonia and River Downs, where cheap and ailing thoroughbreds often demand even more shoeing care than stakes champions, Tex Cauthen soon established a reputation as a member of the horseshoeing elite.

Cauthen did not cut off his studies when he left school at Michigan State. He continued to read veterinary and training manuals, studying the endless angulations and infirmities of horses in the hope of finding some minuscule shoeing adjustments that could ease the problems of his clients' horses. Recognizing his commitment to the art, trainers began looking to him for more than horseshoes. For the shoeing fee that was then $18 per horse and has now reached $27, they also hoped to share Tex's knowledge. They frequently asked for his advice. Sometimes they asked for miracles.

Once, for example, a trainer with a slightly embarrassed grin led a horse out of a stall and showed him to Tex. The colt's ankles were splayed far apart, but his pigeon toes curled so far inward that they almost touched. He seemed an unlikely candidate for walking steadily, much less running around a track.

"We couldn't straighten this dude out with a crowbar," said Tex. "You sure you even want me to bother shoeing him?"

"He's well bred, so the owner has high hopes for him." The trainer laughed. "As long as he feels that way, I'll keep collecting my eighteen dollars a day for training him."

"Then I might as well take my eighteen dollars for shoeing him," said Tex. Astonishingly, the malformed animal went on to race for three years. He even won a small stakes race in Ohio. Cauthen could presumably bask in some of that glory, but it isn't his style. "I don't think we helped that horse as much as he helped us," he says. "He reminded us how little we know."

Just as trainers welcomed Tex as a confidant and friend, they welcomed the little kid who often followed on the morning rounds of the stables. Steve loved to get up with his father, go to the barns at 5:00 A.M., and stay until about 8:00, when he would get a ride to grammar school. At home and in school, Steve sometimes showed the restless, mischievous spirit that Teddy Cleveland called "meanness"; Myra Cauthen remembers a harrowing shopping trip in which Steve grabbed a glass jug off a shelf and teasingly threatened to drop it on the floor unless he was rewarded with some treat. But around the barns, nobody recalls much about Steve except the quiet, rapt attention he devoted to the morning routine. "He didn't get in the way," trainer Jim Sayler recalls. "It seemed like he just wanted to be sure not to miss anything."

Lonnie Abshire recalls those mornings vividly, because they were among the brightest of his training career: the star of his stable was the kind of thoroughbred rarely found at Latonia—a versatile big-league stakes winner named Slade. In full stride driving to a finish line, Slade was as wonderful a sight as Abshire had ever known. But like many good horses, he was too spirited to be handled easily around the barn. Stable hands did not volunteer to enter his stall or walk him around the shed row as he tugged violently at his shank. So it struck Abshire as peculiar one morning when Slade was displaying his temper—and the one figure in the barn who stood by without a trace of a flinch was Tex Cauthen's little kid.

"I can understand how kids might be scared of some things in their lives," says Steve. "But it never did occur to me to be scared of a horse."

In a whimsical mood, Abshire looked at Slade and then at Steve. "Hey, Steve," he kidded, "you got your riding boots on?"

"Yup."

"You want to ride this dude?"

"Yup."

"OK, put the tack on him, boys. You sure you can do it, Steve?"

"Yup."

Suddenly Abshire stopped. Throwing this pleasant kid up onto the most headstrong stallion at Latonia might not turn out to be so funny. The trainer hesitated, then decided to forget the whole thing. But Steve was so excited that he kept pleading, and finally Abshire went along. Steve proceeded to mount Slade and walk him around the barn. As he made his first circuit of the shed row, Slade was snorting, throwing his great head back, baring his teeth. Abshire shuddered slightly as he watched. Then he glanced up at Steve and the trainer's eyes widened in amazement. Steve was laughing at Slade.

The kid was seven years old.

Eight

"Dad, I want to be a race rider."

The skinny baby-faced kid was 12 when he first uttered the words. The early years in barn and pasture, stables and 4-H clubs had laid the foundation for his ambition. The fact that he was growing slowly made the dream all the more plausible. But before you even think about where the words would lead Steve Cauthen or how his father would react to them, it is worthwhile to dwell briefly on the bald fact of Steve's age.

Twelve years old. Junior high. A time, perhaps, for finding the first book that transforms tedious classroom drills into reading for pleasure and discovery. A time for after-school activities, whether they turn out to be sports or clubs or hanging around candy stores with the crowd. A time for the first boy-girl parties, for shyness and silliness and spin the bottle. Twelve is an age for exploration, not ambition. Grade-school visions of becoming doctors or detectives or football stars give way to a vague uncertainty about the future. Perhaps the grand plans will be rekindled later, as grades and energy and money begin to tell kids how far they can go; or they may be lost forever, replaced by more modest goals like going into the service, raising a family, making ends meet. But such alternatives can be faced later. Twelve is not the age for them. It is a time between childish dreams and growing-up pragmatism, a time when there is no need to hurry into anything.

But Steve Cauthen wanted to be a race rider. Despite his stature, he was an all-around athlete, skilled at baseball, basketball, and football. Although he was not a leader he was popular in school, partly because of his knack for humor and nonsense: he and brother Doug won several prizes for dressing up in the funniest costumes for Halloween and other occasions. But Steve's greatest joys came when he was laughing at a fiery stallion like Slade, breaking a yearling for some friend of his father, or winning a ribbon at a 4-H horse show. And there was an urgency in those experiences that wouldn't let him pause and drift and simply be 12 years old.

"When everyone else was running in a pack, I went along," says Steve. *"But even when I was very young, I knew I wanted more than that. I was always a little bored with what was going on. I knew there was more than going to movies or dances or listening to records. I wanted to look ahead. And that's when I told my dad what I really wanted to do."*

It never occurred to Tex Cauthen to dismiss Steve's hope as a youthful folly. Tex had lived the dream himself and watched it bloom in his son, and he sensed that it was right. When Steve put it into words, Tex's mind raced over all the wise counsel he hoped to provide, all the steps that he would eventually suggest for Steve's education as a horseman. Then he stopped himself and reacted in the most basic terms. "I think it's a good idea and I'll help you, on two conditions," he said. "First, don't ever let it swell your head or change you as a person. And second, promise that you'll give it up if you start to grow too big. The minute you have to start starving yourself to make riding weight, you'll have to look for something else to do with your life."

Tex's caution was understandable. Around the tracks, he had seen too many of the vomiting rituals, desperate diets, and flimsy rationalizations that riders use to prolong their years in the saddle. He had seen massive depression alter the lives of rider friends, and he had seen near suicides. He was determined not to condemn his son to that kind of punishment for a dream.

But if nature was willing to go along with Steve, so was his father. "If you're going to try it," Tex told Steve, "you might as well try to be the best. There are a lot of fine points that some riders learn very late in their careers—or never learn at all. I can show you some of them. And what I can't show you, some of my friends probably can. Just pay attention. And be ready to work at it."

In recent years several prominent horsemen have organized schools for the training of young jockeys. Some trainers have met with success in such efforts, but no one has ever devised a curriculum quite as specialized and intensive as the one Tex and his friends set up for young Steve. "And the best thing about it," says Steve, "was that it never stopped being fun. I'll always owe my dad for the tips he gave me. But I'm even more grateful for the love that came along with the advice. Whenever I really needed boosting up, my dad or my mom was there to give it."

The grade-school stage of Steve's racing education was completed years before he made his decision to be a rider. In the family barn he learned how to groom a horse. He knew how to bathe a horse with sponge and detergent and then use a currycomb to wipe away the natural lather, grease, and dandruff that can dull an animal's coat and clog his pores. He could apply the standing leg bandages that keep a horse from kicking himself or suffering other superficial wounds in the stall. And he could wield a brush and a rub rag with great energy to bring a horse's coat to a fine dappled sheen.

These are standard grooming techniques, but they are not to be underestimated. Because of the low-paying, rootless structure of the racing industry, many trainers have difficulty hiring a full staff of adult stable hands who can perform all grooming tasks flawlessly; many jockeys advance far into their careers without ever learning some of the basic day-to-day needs of their horses. An understanding of grooming is one quality that helps to separate the complete horseman from the little man who happens to fit on a horse's back. Caring for horses also has a lot to do with caring *about* horses, and when that becomes second nature, as it did for young Steve, a rider enjoys a forward jump of several furlongs in his trade.

The Cauthen luck with horses took a turn for the better in Walton. With a few dollars to spend at last, the family bought some decent cheap horses and bred and raised some even nicer ones. Their best product, bred by Myra, was a daughter of the unfashionable sire Bernborough out of a cheap mare named Sob Story. The filly, Rough Story, won several races. Another Cauthen-bred horse, Rough March, was sold for a relative windfall price of $9,000—in cash, not on the cuff. Steve got to work around those nice thoroughbreds and appreciate their value and the care they demanded. He also became the proud possessor of several ponies of his own. In one of his first television appearances in New York, an ABC interview with Howard Cosell, Steve later recalled the story of his first pony. Nervous and anxious to please, Steve was uncharacteristically stentorian in the telling. Watching at home in Walton, his brothers thought he was hysterically funny. So Doug and Kerry made their own tape recording, with Doug imitating Cosell and Kerry playing Steve. Somehow that tape tells more about the Cauthen kids' approach to horses and fame than the original interview.

"The American public wants to know," Doug begins, "how a young man like you could learn such responsibility and maturity . . ."

"Well, sir," drawls Kerry, "when I was five my dad gave me this pony. And he looked at me and he said, 'Steve-eh, you better take good care of this pony.'"

"I think that will be enough, Steve," Doug interrupts in Cosellian tones. But Kerry rambles right on.

"My dad said to me, 'Steve-eh, ah don't want to find this pony dead in no ditch, you understand?' And I said, 'Yes sir, I'll take real good care of him, I promise.' And my daddy said . . ."

"Yes, Steve, well, that's a wonderful story," says Doug. "The children of this country should listen to that. And now, it's time to sign off, so ABC can bring us the annual arm-wrestling championships from . . ."

Doug and Kerry dissolve into gales of laughter at the end of the tape, and Tex and Myra laugh along with them each time they hear it. The Cauthens laugh at anything that smacks of myth or legend about Steve. And they are well aware that Steve's early education had a lot less to do with rules and lectures about ponies than it did with an unspoken family understanding about the importance and excitement of the horse.

To view the classroom where a big part of Steve's riding education took place, a visitor must enter the barn behind the Cauthen house and climb up two sets of small and well-worn ladders. There, in the cramped, low-ceilinged loft, a set of reins still dangles from a nail in the wall. Steve once spent hundreds of hours with such reins, until it became second nature to tie them, measure them, and feel them in his hands—an extension of himself into an imaginary horse's mouth. Handling those old reins, you suspect that they have been left there—like the upstairs room in the house that remains pretty much as Steve left it, ready to welcome him back—as a kind of memorial to his learning years. But then Tex reminds you that there is no real reason for them to be taken down, because Steve was still practicing on them until the day he left for the racetrack. And 600 or so winners later, he just might want to practice on them again some time when he is home.

Like many farm children, the Cauthen boys always felt an attraction to the loft—a place for play and solitude as well as a scene of farming chores. When Steve was eight, he once carried some mischievous game too far and fell from an outside window of that loft. Myra was in the kitchen making dinner at the time, and from her window she saw him crash. First she let out a yell.

Then, ignoring the door a few feet away, she vaulted across a counter and through the window. She dropped six feet to the ground without breaking stride and raced to Steve. The kid was unhurt, and within seconds he was laughing at his mother's athletic feat. Then he clambered back up the ladders to resume his games.

The loft was where Steve learned to whip. Soon after he decided to become a jockey, Tex showed him the fundamentals of holding reins and whip, and switching the stick from hand to hand without losing control of the reins. "But showing doesn't mean much," Tex warned. "You've got to do it so often that you can hit a horse just the way you want to, every time, without even thinking about it."

Tex was right. Whipping a racehorse is not merely a technique. It is an art—and one that is much misunderstood. Cheering a furious driving finish from the grandstand, many fans assume that the jockey who hits a horse hardest and most frequently is the one will get the most from his mount. But some horses respond only to certain kinds of whip strokes, some actually sulk when whipped too hard—and no horse benefits when a jockey flails so hard with the whip that he upsets the balance and fluidity of the stride. Like most aspects of riding, whipping doesn't have much to do with raw strength. It is a matter of timing, balance, and sensitivity.

Hard-riding Oklahoman Bobby Ussery, for example, was known for years as the wildest whip rider in New York. Horseplayers and sportswriters often rhapsodized about how Ussery became a blur of churning motion in the saddle as he virtually terrified a tiring horse into lunging toward the wire. Ussery didn't mind the reputation: "Me without a whip," he liked to joke, "would be like a sheriff without a gun."

But in quieter moments, Bobby would encourage friends to view films of some of his supposedly punishing stretch drives. "Watch me closely," he would say, "and count the number of times I hit this poor son of a gun." People would draw breath and prepare to count the rat-a-tat beats. And then Ussery would break up laughing: on close examination it would turn out that he had waved the whip near the horse's eyes, thrust his hands furiously back and forth in rhythm with his mount's stride—and never actually struck the horse. "It's great to be able to hit a horse the right way," Ussery said. "But it's even better to know when not to hit him." The great whip rider took special delight in one of his most famous rides, the 1968 Derby aboard Dancer's Image. In that controversial race, Bobby dropped his whip at the head of the stretch and still finished first—although the colt was later disqualified because of an illegal pain-killer in his system.

Steven Cauthen was to learn how Ussery had felt in that Derby during one of his own memorable afternoons. On April 7, 1977, still almost a month shy of his 17th birthday, Steve won the first five races on the Aqueduct program. He finished out of the money in the sixth, but in the seventh, young trainer Jose Martin hoisted him aboard an odds-on favorite, the solid stretch runner Donizetta. Steve had a very good chance to win six races in one day.

The list of men who had won six races on a New York card before Cauthen reads like an honor roll: Shoemaker, Cordero, and Canadian brothers Ron and Rudy Turcotte, the apprentice sensation of a decade before, Mike Venezia, and old-timer

Alf Robertson. Steve had already equaled the record once, in January. Now he had a chance to become the first rider ever to accomplish the feat twice.

The record danced out of Cauthen's mind as he guided Donizetta down the backstretch in seventh place. He was preoccupied with his instructions—Martin had told him to keep the horse far back until he felt he absolutely had to make a move—and with the field that was strung out in front of him. As the jockeys on the leaders roused their horses into the stretch, Steve was still biding his time. With only a eighth of a mile to go, Donizetta remained in last place.

Finally Steve inched forward over his horse's neck, signaling Donizetta that it was time. Preparing to start whipping, the kid reached down to take a new hold on the reins that had grown slippery on the wet day. Then it happened. The whip slipped through his fingers and dropped harmlessly to the track. While thousands shouted for him to urge the heavily backed favorite to victory, Steve found himself without a whip to do it with.

It could have been an embarrassing interlude in a brilliant day of riding. But Steven had no time to consider that. Almost by instinct, he began to ride as if he had never learned to carry a stick at all. He scrubbed the reins on the horse's neck, then slapped his mount a few times on the shoulder with his hand. And it was enough. Five lengths behind the leaders in midstretch, Donizetta won going away by almost three lengths. The kid had made history with his second six-winner day.

In the jockeys' room he was encircled by interviewers, and he patiently described how good he felt. Someone mentioned the lost whip, which most observers hadn't noticed. "Yup," said Steve. "I just dropped it." No one pressed the point and Cauthen, smiling, walked to the shower to wipe away the last of the afternoon's dirt and mud.

"You sure hate to drop a stick in front of all those people. It's not supposed to happen—that's what all the practicing is about. But the embarrassment is a lot less," Steve adds quietly, *"when you don't happen to get beat."*

Young Steve practiced his whipping at every opportunity. When his days were too occupied by galloping horses or going to school, he sometimes awoke in the middle of the night and climbed into the loft. There he would sit astride a bale of hay, fingering the reins on the wall, passing his stick from hand to hand and snapping it down onto the hay with a crisp, economical motion of the wrist. Gradually he reached a point where, with either hand, he could strike the hay in almost the same place every time. His margin of error dwindled to an eighth of an inch—as close to perfection as he would ever need to be aboard a racehorse in full stride.

Hay in Walton costs about $2.50 a bale, and Steve's constant slashing chewed up scores of bales. During one long evening practice session, Steve was engrossed in switching the stick when he sensed someone nearby. He looked up to see his father standing behind him. "What are you watching?" he asked. "Am I doing something wrong?"

"Nope," said Tex Cauthen. "I was just wondering if you'll ever be worth all these bales of hay you're beating to pieces."

"Sure hope so," said Steve. Then the whip was rising and snapping downward again, always hitting the precise spot that represented a horse's flank in Steve's mind. Tex stood by for quite a long time, studying the deep neat gashes that the well-aimed whip was carving into the hay. Then he climbed soundlessly down the ladders and went back into the kitchen. Feeling good, he opened himself a can of beer.

Nine

"The horse weighs one thousand and I weigh ninety-five," says Steve. *"So I guess I'd better get him to cooperate."*

If the hayloft was Steve's classroom, the farms and tracks around Walton were his laboratories. Many aspects of riding can be studied and practiced and even diagramed, but rapport with the thoroughbred can be achieved only through an ephemeral series of nonverbal, nonscientific experiences—trial and error at 35 miles per hour. Similarly, many of Steve's skills can be described in conventional physical and mental terms; he wins because he has balance and brains and knowledge. But when horsemen try to account for his amazing ability to get horses to "cooperate," even precise and hardheaded people tend to grope vaguely for the right words.

"He's got great hands."

"He has that special touch."

"The kid is a natural."

The phrases are grand and the compliments well intended, but they leave a listener with the haunting, unsatisfied feeling that no one really knows quite how to capture the Cauthen brand of cooperation with the thoroughbred. And maybe that is as it should be. Perhaps it is essential to the Cauthen phenomenon that somewhere between the fundamentals absorbed in the loft and living room and the subtle finishing touches that would later be applied with stopwatches and other sophisticated tools of the racetrack itself, there is a clouded area that defies rational explication.

If textbook-style learning was all there was to it, every kid who was ever born small and interested could presumably reach out for what Steve has found. But only he has ever accomplished so much so quickly on horseback, and so he is entitled to that one mist-shrouded, intensely personal region into which even the shrewdest of his horseman friends cannot really venture. The quality of genius is supposed to have some mystery about it.

O. J. Simpson, perhaps the most gifted athlete who has ever run with a football, expressed the sense of mystery as well as anyone in sports. At the height of his career, after he had set most of pro football's rushing records and translated them into a lucrative media career that would support him long after the last twisting yard had been gained, Simpson was talking about his heir apparent as ball-carrying champion, young Walter Payton of the Chicago Bears. "Walter's got the special ingredient," said O.J. "He's an insane runner."

It was the supreme compliment. Like those who have watched Cauthen, Simpson realized that beyond natural speed and stamina and the clever feints and maneuvers of his craft, there is a quality that cannot be developed or taught. There are only split seconds of difference between the athlete who decides when to cut or accelerate and then does it —and the one who does it without ever having to make the decision. O.J. called it insane, and he meant that it was one step beyond thinking. People around Steve Cauthen call it natural, and they are talking about pretty much the same thing.

In order to explore even the fringes of the mystery of Cauthen's talent, it is probably best to go back to that first childhood ride on the fiery Slade and Steve's subsequent rides on whatever roguish and intractable horses he encountered in northern Kentucky and southern Ohio. Think of the process as laboratory work, field experimentation— trial and error—and you find at least a beginning of a definition of his communication with his mounts: the kid was always ready to try.

Bill Shoemaker, the American-born jockey with whom young Steve is most frequently compared, is another genius who keeps his secrets to himself. Questioned about feel or touch with horses, the winner of more than 7000 races resorts to laconic phrases, easy generalizations. But in his autobiography, *The Shoe*, Shoemaker recalls being a 16-year-old apprentice on a California farm—and his message is about being ready to try.

"When I started breaking yearlings," writes Shoe, "I couldn't wait to get thrown off for the first time. It was a badge of merit or courage to be thrown off. It didn't happen for a couple of days, and I was getting a little disappointed that a horse hadn't bucked me off. But then one did, and after that I got busted forty times a day, and every time a horse threw me off, I thought it was fun."

Fun may be a strange word for the experience. Tex Cauthen doesn't recall any great mirth in his first spills from the bucking horses of old Henry Collins, and Steve doesn't laugh when he speaks of his own early crashes. But if falling wasn't exactly fun for the Cauthens, it was certainly accepted as a part of what they were doing, even a part of what they were. "I've been watching Steve since he was twelve or thirteen," says Kentucky trainer Jim Sayler. "And I've never seen him turn down a chance to gallop a horse. I've seen him get bucked ten feet in the air and slammed to the ground. And the next thing I'd know, he'd brush himself off and say, 'I think I know what went wrong. When do I get back up and try this horse again?'"

Sayler is a veteran horseman who has ridden in rodeos and races and trained his share of horses who were ill-tempered, dangerous, and worst of all, slow. His brother Bernie is a steady rider on the Kentucky-Ohio circuit. The Saylers have known long summers when purse money never seemed to catch up with expenses, and winters when tracks like Latonia became blocks of ice that froze the horsemen out of desperately needed income. These are men who have paid their dues in broken bones and shattered hopes, and they do not bestow praise casually on any kids who arrive at trackside with illusions about being race riders. But when they speak of young Cauthen, these tight-lipped hardboots tend to sound like Hollywood press agents.

"We had to work for years to develop traits that come naturally to Steve," says Jim Sayler. "Almost from the time he started galloping horses, I've watched true nut cases become kind when Steve took hold of the reins. I'm not sure what the secret is. Maybe Steve is so calm and relaxed on a horse that the horse senses it and begins to feel the same way."

Occasionally writers have sought more rigorous definitions of this mystery between man and horse. The late Wilhelm Müseler, a great German equestrian, once wrote a book with a challenging title that seemed to minimize vague secrets in favor of a crisp Teutonic order: *Riding Logic.* The work is concerned with dressage and show jumping, not racing, and it was first translated into English back in 1937, before Tex Cauthen was old enough to begin his study of horses. But even today, the author's preface seems to defy some of the very "logic" that he sought. It also seems very much in tune with what Jim Sayler and other Kentuckians saw in young Steve Cauthen.

"Anybody can learn to ride, for riding is nothing but a skill," wrote Müseler. "But it can be made an art. And who would not be an artist? . . . The end of all schooling and dressage is perfect harmony between man and mount—Beauty. The horse must show that he feels comfortable and the rider must not betray how hard it is to achieve this!"

Push the bookish analysis one step farther and you might arrive at William Faulkner, whose subject was the soul and not the saddle, but whose terrain was the same "dark and bloody ground" that spawned the first Confederate soldiers who got the Cauthen family into the horse business. In *Absalom, Absalom!* the novelist told of the demonic hero Thomas Sutpen, locked in a towering and doomed struggle against his enemies and the wilderness and his own tragic flaws. In one metaphor, Faulkner captured a truth not only about man and life but about man on horseback: a man "compromising with his dream and his ambition like you must with a horse which you take across country over timber, which you control only through your ability to keep the animal from realizing that actually you cannot, that actually it is the stronger."

This would be heady stuff in conversations over coffee in the Latonia track kitchen, where literature is represented by a crudely lettered sign over the steam table: "Silverware is not medicine. Do not take it after meals." But this aspect of the Cauthen story merits the resonance of other men in other contexts who have been fascinated by similar mysteries. More important, Faulkner's words on the subject find a poignant echo in those of a teenaged jockey who has never read such books—but has perhaps inherited some of their indomitable spirit.

"I didn't have any magic touch," says Steve. *"I got thrown off or run off with plenty of times. But maybe I was lucky that I was little and didn't have much strength. When a horse is running off, out of control, the natural temptation is to try to wrestle him or drag him to a stop. But I knew from the start that the horse was too strong for me. I could never overpower him. So I was always trying to outsmart him."*

During his 13th summer, Steve worked on a farm for trainer Lonnie Abshire. One morning Lonnie was exercising Latin Image, the roughest and most ornery beast in his care at the time. As Abshire pulled the horse to a stop, Steve was standing nearby. "This is the kind of dude you have to be real careful with," Abshire called to Steve. "You got to keep your eye on him every minute. You can never relax." As he spoke, Lonnie relaxed and looked over at Steve. Just then Latin Image bucked and tossed Abshire from the saddle. The trainer hit the ground with a thud, injuring his back. Steve rushed over and helped him up. For a while he listened quietly as the man he called Uncle Lonnie berated himself for his own carelessness. Then, when his friend had quieted down and assured him that he was not too badly hurt, the kid spoke up: "Can I ride this horse tomorrow morning?"

Abshire agreed, but not without hesitation and many warnings. "Don't forget what happened to me," he called as Steve galloped away from him on Latin Image. "Keep your eye on him." A few minutes later, Abshire's fears were realized. Latin Image galloped back to the barn without a rider.

Then, just as the trainer was preparing to go looking for him, Steve appeared on foot, grinning sheepishly. "I'm sorry, I forgot what you told me," he said. "The horse was going along fine when I spotted at a rabbit coming out of the woods. The second I turned my head to look, this horse knew it—and I was on the ground." The kid pursed his lips. If he was bruised or shaken, it wasn't apparent. "Don't worry, though, Uncle Lonnie," he said firmly. "I'll handle him OK the next time."

"And that's just what he did," recalls Abshire. "You hardly ever had to tell Steve anything twice. And you never had to tell him a third time."

Frank Tours and a few other old Latonia hands had been talking about Tex Cauthen's kid for years. But most of the weathered horsemen around small racetracks tend to dismiss rumors about prodigies. They have seen too many kids grown heavy or swellheaded before their futures ever had a chance to happen, and in any case, there is little time for contemplating anyone's future when rent and feed bills are past due. Idle chatter wasn't going to convince anybody at Latonia that the blacksmith's kid was a race rider. He would have to show them.

The first horse that Steve was allowed to "breeze" at the track was named Be a Saint. The name was not particularly well chosen. "Horses don't get shipped to this level because of their great behavior records," says Abshire. "A lot of them have ailments that hurt them most of the time, which doesn't do much for their dispositions. Others are just naturally mean or speed-crazy. Naturally we all wanted Steve to do well in his first breeze and we picked out a horse that wasn't too hard to handle. But that didn't mean that he couldn't be trouble."

Breezing is the advanced stage of learning to exercise thoroughbreds. An exercise rider first learns to gallop a horse, then to breeze. In a gallop, a horse is eased along at a fairly leisurely clip, with the rider standing up in the stirrups and maintaining a firm, restraining hold on the reins. In a breeze, the rider lowers himself over his mount as if in a race and encourages him to show speed over a relatively short distance.

Contrary to some impressions, galloping can actually be more difficult than breezing. A thoroughbred is bred and raised to show speed; every stage of his education points toward the moment when he will be asked to run as fast and far as he can in competition. So when a horse is galloping on the track, and particularly when he sees other horses running past him, he may be inclined to lunge against the big in his mouth, lengthen his stride and burst into full speed. The person on his back must be sensitive to the first hint that a horse has such running in mind—or he or she will be in the hazardous and embarrassing position of being "run off with."

Controlling a horse at a gallop requires a firm and steady grip on the reins; you do not meet many exercise riders, male or female, with weak handshakes. But as Cauthen emphasizes, strength alone could never be enough. A good rider transmits his message to his horse's mouth subtly and soothingly, with a minimum of struggle. Challenge a horse to a test of strength and you can be certain of only one thing. He'll win.

In a breeze, restraint is less of a problem. Instead, the rider must be most concerned with how fast he is going. Training a horse is a profession demanding great patience. Before he can be tested for speed at all, a horse must build up his muscles and respiratory system in long gallops. Then, in a painstaking series of breezes, he may be asked to show small increments of all-out speed. But if he happens to work out at a pace that his body is not fit enough to stand, the entire course of his progress can be upset. Hurt or sick or merely sour of disposition, he may force his trainer to go back and rebuild him all over again. "Try to hurry a horse," a backstretch axiom maintains, "and he'll find a way to make you wait."

This omnipresent danger places considerable pressure on a rider. If a trainer has a horse fit enough to run a half mile in 52 seconds, and a rider allows him to complete the distance in 48 seconds, the training program can be ruined. The rider can also find himself seeking other employment. Perhaps the most famous case of a mistimed workout occurred shortly after Steve Cauthen attended his first Derby. The winner, Chateaugay, was masterfully trained by Jimmy Conway, a man who always knows just how much work his horses require. After his Derby triumph, Conway estimated that Chateaugay could use a nice, easy one-mile breeze before he raced in the Preakness, the second race of the Triple Crown series. But surrounded by reporters and television cameras on the busling Pimlico backstretch, a normally reliable exercise boy seemed to succumb to the bright lights. As an anquished Conway stood by helplessly with stopwatch in hand, the boy worked out Chateaugay in near record time.

The newspapers were ablaze with reports about how brilliantly Chateaugay was training, but the crafty Conway knew better. A few days later, drained by the needless effort he had expended in the workout, Chateaugay finished a poor second in the Preakness. When the colt returned to New York—after Conway slowed down his training again—he reaffirmed his superiority by winning the Belmont Stakes. But the victory was tinged with sadness, because it only underscored the fact that one overzealous workout at Pimlico had probably deprived a worthy horse and a brilliant horseman of the achievement of the Triple Crown.

There were no Triple Crown candidates on the Latonia backstretch in 1974. But Tex Cauthen and his trainer friends were still cautious about entrusting 14-year-old Steve with a horse to breeze. "Steve always figures he was ready to do anything," says Tex. "Most of the time, he has turned out to be right. But I always preferred to err on the side of letting him learn too slowly rather than too fast. It's nice to be as certain as you can be about something like that."

Lonnie Abshire was certain as he hoisted Steve onto Be a Saint. "Just let him go an easy three-eights in about forty," he told Steve. Be a Saint breezed smoothly down the stretch and Abshire clicked his watch: 39 3/5 seconds. Steve was an exercise rider.

Soon the skeptics around Latonia were paying attention. "I have a horse that's been running away with my hundred-and-sixty-pound exercise boys," one trainer challenged Abshire. "Think that kid can handle him?"

"Try him," said Lonnie. Steve galloped the horse easily, and his reputation continued to build. The only thing the kid couldn't do, the old-timers joked, was work a horse during the last hour of training on a weekday morning. By that time, he had hitched a ride out of the stable area so he would be on time for his classes at junior high.

"*I learned a lot around Latonia and I usually did a good job,*" says Steve. "*But I had my share of problems, too. I remember those tough horses that I galloped OK, but I remember others that wheeled and propped and threw me plenty of times. You don't learn this business without having your share of horses run off with you.*"

"*What crosses your mind when a horse is running off with you on a crowded racetrack?*" he is asked. "*It must be pretty scary.*"

"*Nope.*" The voice is as flat and matter-of-fact as it must have been on the morning when a seven-year-old first climbed up on Slade. "*You just try to keep your horse between the fences and not run over anybody. You're not scared. Just busy.*"

Ten

"I did all right in school," says Steve. "But it was hard to concentrate, because my mind was always on horses. I realized that learning was important. But what I wanted to learn about was horses."

Mystery is essential to horse racing. If every horse ran exactly the same way in every race, results would be foreordained and horseplayers would have nothing to bet on. If every foal grew up to duplicate the abilities of its parents, there would be no fascination in the quest for the obscure genetic matchup or "nick" that produces a winner, and a lot of expensive mineral-rich farmland could be made available for shopping centers. In betting on horses as well as raising or racing them, the believer in sure things is not only a fool, but one who is missing much of the delight of the game. One of the genuine pleasures of racing is the constant element of surprise—the reminder that there will always be one more thing that can't be figured out.

This is why the impact of a Secretariat or a

Seattle Slew or a Cauthen is more than the sum of victories, records, and money won. The joy of watching a champion derives in part from the knowledge that thousands of other horses and people have enjoyed similar abilities and inspired similar hopes, only to fall short. The quality that sets the champions apart—whether it is buried deep in the heart of a racehorse or curled magically through the long fingers of a teenaged rider—is all the more fascinating because it defies precise descripion.

Like many good mysteries, however, racing's secrets lie disarmingly close to its day-to-day realities. Almost every time you think you are probing into wondrous "natural" gifts, you find yourself stumbling across some basic, tediously acquired skill. Racetrackers usually develop their magic the hard way.

The most closely studied genius in racing, for example, may well be trainer H. Allen Jerkens. A large, soft-spoken man who accepts success with much the same easy modesty as Cauthen, Jerkens happens to be the greatest living horse trainer in America—and probably in the world. Backstretch habitués are often drawn to Jerkens's barns at Belmont or Hialeah to search out the tricks that make horses of modest breeding or ability run like champions for the trainer. Occasionally the visitor seizes a hint of something special: a horse en route to the track for a workout is suddenly summoned back to the barn because of some slight distress sign that only the trainer has spotted; another colt receives an unorthodox breeze on the very morning when he is supposed to be resting up for an afternoon race. But for the most part, the Jerkens barn operates like any other well-run outfit, and the outsider who wants to praise Jerkens falls back on ephemeral superlatives.

"There are three categories of horse trainer," says Jerkens's friend and rival Phil Johnson. "Bad ones, good ones, and Allen." Dr. Manuel Gilman, the state-employed veterinarian who examines all the racehorses and horsemen in New York, adds perhaps the most enduring epithet: "Allen Jerkens is part horse."

But just as you begin to accept this sort of supernatural explanation, you notice the little finite things. While other trainers assign stable hands to dish out meals to horses, Jerkens does it himself, adding or subtracting from the rations like a gourmet chef, making sure that each animal eats exactly what he needs. While others lament about the difficulty of finding skilled and loyal help, Jerkens raises salaries and improves working conditions so he can attract and keep some of the best stable hands in the game. In the late mornings and again at evening feeding time, when other trainers have long since repaired to golf courses or relaxing cocktail hours, Jerkens can still be found at the barn, attending to some final detail. Part horse, he is all horseman. And so the elusive quality of genius begins to look very much like hard work.

It is much the same with Steve Cauthen, "the natural." Once he had proved his knack for galloping horses before the hard critics at Latonia, young Steve was determined to continue his education in whatever graduate courses the track happened to offer. Beginning jockeys are called apprentices for a reason; they are supposed to learn while they ride. Steve didn't want it that way. He hoped to absorb the apprentice lessons before he was even old enough to enter a race. And a life of struggling on the track had made his father an ideal man to run a seminar for him.

"I had done a lot of thinking about some topics

that many modern riders don't discuss," says Tex Cauthen. "I guess the most obvious was wind resistance. Some very good jockeys ride fairly high over their mounts, moving around quite a bit. Some get very good results, so I don't mean to criticize their styles. But it's only common sense that if you're down low and still over a horse, you're going to create less drag and give him that much better chance."

That brand of common sense appealed to Steve. The more he rode, the lower he seemed to poise his slim body over his mounts. Unlike the "whoop-de-doo" riders who dominate modern racing, he tried to eliminate all but the most necessary motion. When Bill Shoemaker broke in as an apprentice in California some 25 years earlier, he was actually criticized for such lack of motion. Horsemen complained that he should be pumping and slashing in the irons like other riders—and it took the first thousand or so Shoemaker winners before they were stilled. Now racetrack people compare Cauthen's seat on a horse to that of the young Shoe. By the time he reached the races, Steve's seat was a subject of awe among some rivals. "He rides so low," marveled Kentucky jockey Jim McCullars, "sometimes I look up at him during a race and I think he must have fallen off."

With characteristic logic, Tex Cauthen also encouraged his son to begin his racing studies at the beginning—the starting gate. Steve was only 12 when Tex first took him out to the starting gate at River Downs; he was a regular visitor at gates for the next few years. The assistant starters, the men who lead horses into the gate and try to keep them calm and aimed in the right direction in the tense seconds before the gate opens, were often friends of the popular local blacksmiths. They were busy, but they found time to answer the polite questions from Tex Cauthen's kid.

"There are a lot of ways a horse can get beat when he should win," says Tex. "But the most common way of all is probably by screwing up at the start. I told Steve to study which riders were too jittery before the start and which ones got caught being too relaxed, leaning back when the doors opened. He also got to see how horses had to be treated as individuals in the gate—just like they do everywhere else. Some have to be soothed, others have to be kept alert. Steve saw that. Some of the things that other kids have to learn by getting left at the post in races, Steve was able to find out ahead of time." It was a valuable shortcut. Some of the best modern "gate boys," including Bobby Ussery and Walter Blum, did not achieve the designation until they were grown-up men. But before he ever raced, Steve was at home in the big metal gate.

To a beginner, a starting gate can be a noisy and forbidding contraption. There is padding on the sides of each stall, and bumpers extend out in front of the gate for several feet to keep horses from lunging into one another as they charge into a race. But there are also large expanses of steel siding and piping that can crush bones all too quickly when a horse acts up and a rider gets hurled against the gate. When a kid on horseback finds the steel doors shut behind and in front of him, the first thing he needs is nerve.

While jockeys and assistant starters position the horses in the stalls of the gate, the official starter watches from a raised platform near the inside rail. The gate is operated by a kind of reverse electricity. The doors are sealed shut by a single current running through them. When the starter feels that the field is ready, he presses the button in his hand. It breaks the circuit and the gates spring open. There is only an infinitesimal chance of malfunction in the machinery, but there is endless room for human error. The starter may not notice that one horse is off balance and unprepared. An assistant starter, perched on the side of a stall and holding a horse's head straight, may hold his grip for a split second too long. Or a jockey may have his weight distributed just poorly enough to slow his mount in the first stride. An adequate gate boy learns to avoid the pitfalls of unreadiness. A very good one knows the hazards so well that he no longer needs to think of them. Instead, he almost becomes a part of the electricity around him, sensing and even anticipating the moment of takeoff. By the time he was 14, Steve was learning the difference.

"I watched a lot of starts," says Steve. "I saw riders who, no matter what they did, never quite seemed to be tied on when the gates opened. Others managed to be ready and get off OK. And a few really helped their horses get out of there. They didn't use any one trick. They knew their horses and they paid attention. I try to do the same thing."

Steve's next stop was the clockers' stand—the outpost on the backstretch of every track where one can find some of the wildest extremes of racing life. The clockers' stand is a place for measuring the speed of horses with precise watches, but it is also the nerve center for the wildest tall tales and rumors. It is a good place to study the sly chicanery and human foibles of men who hope to keep the speed to horses to themselves until after a bet has been cashed. It is also perhaps the best place in which to take a crash course in a crucial element of racing—knowledge of pace.

Clockers are usually employed by the trade paper the *Daily Racing Form*, which prints workouts for the aid of handicappers. Some are employed by racetracks, and a few work for themselves, always hoping to spot a fast horse one race before the public does. The profession is a specialized one: the clocker must identify each horse as it enters the track, begin timing it when it breaks off from a gallop into a serious breeze, and then records its time. Some trainers help the clockers along by alerting them to a horse that is about to breeze. But many do not. A horseman who has spent months getting a horse ready for a victory often prefers to let the horse arrive at the finish line as a surprise—raising the price that he can collect on his bet.

As a result, the clockers' stand can be a den of confusion, particularly to an outsider. Some regulars may know exactly what is happening on the track and prepare to inform the public. Others may know but plan not to tell. And still others may be genuinely puzzled about the identity of whatever plainly marked bay horse just flew past at a brilliant clip. In all cases, varying degrees of knowledge and confusion are masked behind idle and intentionally uninformative banter. As a rule, a clockers' stand is not a hospitable setting for a youngster who wants to ask questions.

But Steve asked, and he got answers. The clockers knew Tex and they knew of his son's ambitions. Perhaps they even sensed that they were playing bit parts in a drama that would long outlive whatever bet they hoped to cash the next week. But most important, they liked the kid. "Most kids could never have learned the way Steve did around the track," says Jim Sayler. "They would have gotten in the way of the normal routine, and somebody would have chased them. But Steve was so polite and enthusiastic, people always wanted to help him. He's the kind of kid every racetracker dreams about having. So he got what he needed."

For an entire summer, Steve checked in at the clockers' stand every day. He watched thousands of horses work out, estimated how fast they were moving, and then checked his guesses against the clockers' watches. After a while, he hardly needed to check the watches. He usually knew just how fast a horse was going. And he was able to apply that skill when he was in the saddle.

Some riders spend entire careers wishing that they had been blessed with the "clock in the head" that marks great judges of pace like Eddie Arcaro, Bill Shoemaker, or Braulio Baeza. At 14, Steve didn't wish. In those long, repetitious hours with the clockers, he virtually installed a clock in his own head.

As Steve's racing education accelerated, his father decided to talk to him about his "other" school. Tex told Steve that if he wanted to start riding as soon as he turned 16 and became eligible for a license, he would have to improve his grades in the time he had left at Walton-Verona.

In junior high, Steve was an average kid and an average student. He liked to play ball and trampoline and prepare his horses for 4-H shows, and he devoted some modest effort to his classes. But once his father had linked his grades to his racing future, Steve took up the challenge. Even while his head was a jumble of starting gates and stopwatches, he managed to hike his high-school marks above a B average. He did have to curtail his hours with his friends, however, because he was in an increasing hurry to get his homework and chores done. He knew that he still had a lot of learning to do.

At some point during each evening of his sophomore year, Steve would close his textbooks and darken his room; it was time for some film study. Through friendly track officials, Tex had acquired almost 100 patrol films of races at Latonia and River Downs. Using a borrowed projector, father and son would play the films backward and forward until they were almost committed to memory. Steve watched how inexperienced riders drove their mounts into positions where they got hopelessly blocked. He saw horses make their moves too soon or too late because jockeys had misjudged the pace of a race. When he had absorbed all the mistakes that he wanted to avoid, he turned his attention to the best rider at River Downs, Larry Snyder. Steve appreciated the way Snyder rode low over his horse, reacted smoothly in tight situations, and saved his horses for victorious rushes through the stretch. He wanted to emulate many of Snyder's skills. It even occurred to him, without cockiness, that he could do better.

"We just about wore those films out," says Tex Cauthen. "In the last few months before his sixteenth birthday, Steve wanted to keep going over things, making sure he wasn't missing anything. It was getting to be a little tense being around him, because he was really getting itchy to ride."

On May 1, 1976, the day that Angel Cordero won the Kentucky Derby with Bold Forbes, Steve turned 16. He was eligible for a jockey's license, eligible to begin the high-speed quest that would eventually carry him past Cordero in the New York jockey standings. "I thought this day would never get here," he told his parents at a birthday dinner.

And throughout the evening, he tended to repeat himself. "I'm ready to start, dad. I'm ready to ride."

"Hell, I knew he was ready," says Tex Cauthen. "By the time that birthday came around, he'd been ready for a long while."

Eleven

"I'm ready. I'm ready." Looking back now, across the hundreds of victories and the awards and the accelerated process of growing up in full public view, it is difficult for Steve or his father or their friends to remember the urgency and edginess in the kid's words. The preparation, after all, had been meticulous. The lessons had been carefully learned. The dues had been paid. And so the first ride in a race was scheduled as just one more step in the progression: first gallop, first breeze, first fall from the saddle—first race. Nothing to get excited about.

Only Myra Cauthen sensed something more. "Steve walked into the paddock trying to look as calm as he could," she says. "But I could see something in his eyes and in the way he moved. My own knees felt a little weak, and suddenly I knew that Steve was feeling the same way. Sure he had the training and experience to do it. But in that moment I forgot all that. I was a mother and Steve

*was a boy who had just turned sixteen. We were
both a little scared."*

The saddling area at Churchill Downs in Louisville is tucked away under the superstructure of
the grandstand, enclosed by wooden boards and
wire-mesh fencing. On warm afternoons it has a
cramped, almost airless quality. The paddock's
fame is largely negative: on Kentucky Derby day
it is so clogged with racing celebrities and media
people that it can become claustrophobic, taking a
severe toll on high-strung horses. More than one
Derby candidate has become unglued in the frantic atmosphere, losing the race before setting foot
on the track. The most famous casualty of the scene
was probably Damascus in 1967. Drained by the
tension of the saddling routine, that hot-blooded
colt ran a weak third in the Derby. Then he won
the Preakness and Belmont Stakes, underlining
the grim fact that he had lost the Triple Crown in
the chaos of the Churchill Downs paddock. So the
saddling area has a secure place in racing history,
as one of the many potential traps that make the
Triple Crown so elusive—and racing so unpredictable.

Twelve days before Steve Cauthen took his
first walk into that paddock, another talented Derby favorite had suffered through the paddock experience. Bert Firestone's Honest Pleasure had
been the odds-on favorite for the 1976 Derby—the
hottest favorite, in fact, since Native Dancer, who
had been upset back in 1953. But Honest Pleasure
had peaked too early in his three-year-old campaign, and by Derby day he was peculiarly vulnerable to the hazards of Churchill Downs. He was
edgy in the paddock and sweaty as he walked onto
the track. The best he could do was a second-place

finish behind the brilliant front-running victor, Bold Forbes.

By May 12, the Derby mobs had long since dispersed. Before the day's first race the paddock was quiet—perhaps a little too still for Myra Cauthen's nerves. But if Steve's mother spotted a flicker of fear in his eyes or a hesitation in his gait, no one else did. Poker-faced and intent on his mount, a $5000 claiming horse called King of Swat, the kid appeared to be all business.

"The horse had been vanned down from Latonia to give me my first shot," Steve says. "We all knew that he was only fit to run about a half mile, and the race was at three-quarters. So nobody expected him to win. And nobody was about to blame me when he didn't."

The bettors certainly expected nothing. King of Swat went to the post at odds of 136–1. When the starting gate opened, Cauthen got him away smoothly in the middle of the pack. Steady and almost motionless, he began to ease the horse toward the leaders. There was no sign of his inexperience.

In the grandstand, Tex Cauthen trained his binoculars on the race and watched in silence. But Myra's knuckles were white around her own field glasses. "Why did I ever let him do this?" she murmured. "Maybe this is all a big mistake. Why did I let him go through with it?" Tex Cauthen didn't answer.

After a quarter of a mile, Steve had King of Swat placed third, within a length of the leader. At the half he was fourth, but only a half-length behind in the tightly bunched field. That first 47 1/5-second, half-mile run could have been the stuff of dreams, stirring youthful visions of a miraculous debut. But Steve knew better. He was not surprised when King of Swat began to tire beneath him, and he did not punish the horse needlessly as he dropped back through the field. There would be plenty of time later for whipping, driving, exciting stretch runs. Now he just wanted to ride his well-beaten mount professionally. King of Swat beat only one horse, another obscure long shot named Master Pip. Steve Cauthen's first mount finished tenth, 16 lengths behind the winner.

"I rode him good," Steve said flatly. "And then he stopped."

"That's right," Tex Cauthen said quietly. "You rode him fine."

"I'll never forget the fear I felt in my stomach during that race," says Myra Cauthen. "But by the time Steve came to the paddock for his second race of the day, everything was different. He was walking a little steadier, smiling a little more confidently. And I started to feel better too. From that point on, I started to get over my worrying about him."

Steve's second mount of the day was another forlorn long shot, a three-year-old maiden named Singing Saint. The odds were 50–1. The race was at one mile and a sixteenth—a little more than one full circuit of the track—so the starting gate was placed in front of the grandstand. The Cauthens got a closeup as Steve again broke well from the gate and moved his mount toward the leaders. Around the first turn he stayed within a neck of the leader. Then, like King of Swat an hour earlier, Singing Saint began to run to his limited capabilities. He dropped back steadily on the backstretch, then continued evenly through the stretch. He finished sixth, beaten by nine lengths.

Steve's performance sent no ripples of conversation through the clubhouse bars or backstretch barns of Churchill Downs. Hardly a day goes by in racing without some new kid at some track making a debut. Such occasions are often marked by cryptic notes at the bottom of the news releases that are distributed daily in track press boxes. Because of limitations in time and space, a young lifetime's dreams are often boiled down into vital statistics and predictable phrases. "Young Gregory, from Rockaway, was brought to the track by his uncle ... Mark was encouraged to try riding by classmates because of his small stature and strong arms ... Steve is a blacksmith's son from Walton, Kentucky ..." Sometimes the notes are dropped into the final paragraphs of a newspaper's racing summary, or filed for future reference in case the kid happens to be the rare one who makes good. The majority are forgotten as quickly as an afternoon's also-rans.

Kentuckians are particularly wary of wide-eyed newcomers with get-rich-quick ambitions. By definition, the Kentucky "hardboot" is a skeptic. He has been trained and hardened through generations filled with more defeats than triumphs, and he knows the odds. Around young horses and young people, he bestows his hopes and opinions sparingly. Youngsters are expected to undergo the same tests of time and disappointment that the hardboot has undergone. Only then will the hardboot squint through sun-wrinkled eyes and nod approval—grudgingly.

A few days after Cauthen's debut, a young trainer named Dan Riesenbeck walked into the racing secretary's office at Churchill Downs and mentioned that he planned to use young Steve on one of his horses. Several old-timers spoke up at once.

"Has your horse got any chance to win?"

"I think so," said Riesenbeck.

"Then you're crazy to ride the kid," said one.

"Let the kid make his mistakes for somebody else," said another. A third listener recalled a familiar Kentucky axiom: "A man can work months to get a horse ready to win a bet for him, and then some kid can screw it up in the last six seconds before the wire." Months later Riesenback was to laugh about such opinions about the kid who was to become a star. But at Churchill Downs that spring such attitudes were very real. And they could have made it hard for even the best young apprentice to get a fast start in his career. Tex Cauthen had done enough homework to understand that, so it was not surprising that he directed Steve toward a track where the competition was slightly less intense and the trainers already knew something of Steve's talent. Five days after his Churchill debut, Steve was riding closer to home at River Downs.

The rules of racing acknowledge the difficulties facing the beginning rider. To make it easier for a newcomer to break in, he is provided with a weight allowance. To compensate for his inexperience, his mounts are required to carry less weight than they would with a veteran jockey. Sometimes the lower weight can help a horse win a race that he would otherwise lose. More important, horsemen often *think* that fewer pounds of lead in the saddlebags will make a difference—and so they give apprentices more opportunities to ride.

The raw beginner is allowed a ten-pound allowance until he wins five races. He continues to carry seven pounds less than veterans until he has won 35 times. Then he rides with a five-pound allowance until a year after the date of his fifth winner. The allowances are noted by asterisks next to the listed weight of a horse in a racing program. Three asterisks indicate a ten-pound allowance, two a seven-pound, and one a five-pound. The asterisks are known as "bugs," and apprentices are called bug boys. Some endure depressingly long months as "triple-bug" riders, searching in vain for those first five winners and sometimes dropping from sight without ever shedding the three asterisks that mark their continued failures. At River Downs, Steve Cauthen remained a triple-bug boy for all of two weeks.

The featured eighth race on May 17 carried a purse of $3800—not small change by River Downs standards. One of the contenders, a stretch runner called Red Pipe, was supposed to carry 113 pounds under the conditions of the race. But Red Pipe's trainer decided to take his chances on an apprentice with a triple bug. Under Steve Cauthen, Red Pipe got into the race with only 103 pounds. Of course, the trainer had a considerable edge when he chose his triple-bug jockey. He was Tommy Bischoff, Myra Cauthen's brother.

The race was a five-and-a-half-furlong sprint. (A furlong is an eighth of a mile.) The track was sloppy. Ordinarily, a wet track favors horses with early speed, if only because come-from-behind horses can become discouraged when they are splattered with great quantities of mud. But Bischoff assured his nephew that Red Pipe would run willingly despite the conditions. He told Steve to let the horse relax and then make one run through the stretch.

In thoroughbred racing, distances are measured off by striped poles along the inside rail of the track, marking each sixteenth of a mile. In charting the progress of a race, distance is always measured from the finish line rather than the start. The half-mile pole, for example, is a half-mile from the finish; the eighth pole denotes that there is an eighth of a mile remaining in the race, and so on. So when a rider plans a charge to the wire with a come-from-behind horse, he usually decides to begin his move at a particular pole. On Red Pipe, Steve Cauthen hoped to launch his bid soon after he passed the three-eighths pole.

Steve remembers the race as clearly as he does the Washington D.C. International. On the backstretch he allowed Red Pipe to meander along far behind his field. At the three-eighths pole, midway on the far turn, he was so far behind that he barely felt the clods of mud that the leaders were kicking back toward him. It was a time when young riders can be forgiven for their doubts, when a race seems to be slipping hopelessly out of reach. But Red Pipe was handling the sloppy track well, striding smoothly and taking a firm hold on the bit in his mouth. Steve felt that good firm feeling in his hands, and he decided to wait a bit longer before asking the horse for speed. He had waited years for his first winner. There was no need to hurry.

"We were way, way out of it," says Steve. "We must have been fifteen lengths out of it at the three-eighths pole. But when we hit the stretch and I finally hit him, the horse really charged. To hit him and have him respond like that was a great feeling." At the eighth pole, Red Pipe was third on the outside, and the track announcer was shouting that he was *"the strong horse, coming on."* Steve didn't hear the call and he didn't need to. *"He really charged home,"* he says. *"I knew he would get home in time."* Red Pipe won by a length and a half, and Bischoff and Tex and Myra were smiling and cheering when Steve galloped him back to the winner's circle. *"A great, great feeling,"* he repeats when he thinks of the race. *"It felt just as good as I'd always dreamed it would."*

Back in the jockeys' room, the older riders knew how the kid was feeling. And they were prepared to share his elation in the initiation rite that greets every young jock on the occasion of his first winner. Steve had been aware of the ritual, but in his excitement he forgot it as he strode through the door. Then the others pounced on him. Most were armed with greasy rags covered with boot polish. Others wielded shaving-cream dispensers or containers of whatever else happened to be wet and sticky. Laughing uproariously, they painted the rookie with polish and lather. Finally he struggled from their grips and stumbled to a mirror. "Man, I look hideous," he cried. Then he stood still, hesitating for a moment to go to the shower and wash. "But I sure feel great."

Steve is often asked about that first victory, and when he retells the story, he tends to mute the jockeys' shouting and mask any lingering emotion. Sometimes he sounds vaguely like a handicapper reading numbers from a *Racing Form* chart book. Frequently, he even adds a flat, matter-of-fact postscript: "The horse paid eight dollars."

The words reveal a wisdom that some racetrackers acquire only over lifetimes. Steve seems to enjoy a built-in sense of perspective about the strange business-sport that is thoroughbred racing —a calm understanding of the fact that one young man's historic milestone may be, for thousands of horseplayers, an immediate matter of what it means at the $2 cashier's window. This kind of overview can be very helpful to a young rider, who otherwise might find himself confused and troubled when the same fans who have just cheered him to a great stakes victory begin booing and cursing after he has lost on an odds-on favorite. But it can be just as valuable to the outsider who wants to savor horse races not only for their present-tense impact but for their place in a wider and more fascinating mosaic. The beauty of racing lies largely in the fact that almost any race can be described with equal accuracy and excitement by saying "He paid eight dollars" or "He fulfilled somebody's dream of a lifetime."

The best horse of our time provides the best example of this. Secretariat's brilliance was easily measured by stopwatches and cash registers. But each time that he set a track record or added another $100,000 to his earnings, the big red colt was also adding to a more romantic, slowly unfolding tale. For Secretariat's story had its genesis three decades before the colt was born, when Christopher Chenery, a man of great wealth and independent spirit, insisted on paying a meager $750 for a slow-footed filly with bloodlines that intrigued him.

Named Hildene, that filly failed as a racehorse and never saw any of her offspring, for she went blind soon after giving birth to her first foal. But Hildene produced a string of champions, justifying Chenery's faith and setting the foundation for his stable. Soon he parlayed her success into purchases of other great mares. One of them, Imperatrice, produced an unraced daughter named Something-royal, who in turn produced Secretariat. Chenery was elderly and infirm by the time Secretariat was conceived and he did not live to see the colt win the Triple Crown. But his daughter, Penny Tweedy Ringquist, knew what his life in racing had meant to him and what he would have wanted. So she held the stable together in the face of huge estate taxes and the caution of legal advisers—and Secretariat became a breathtaking monument to her determination and the dreams that had first swirled to life around an old blind mare. Racetrackers often called Secretariat a "today horse"—

a viscerally exciting athelete, a crowd grabber, a media hero. But he was also a horse with a history. The two elements often go together in racing. Very nicely.

Light-years from the grandeur of Secretariat, in the second race at River Downs on May 19, 1976, was a story with similar outlines. Some five years earlier, while her oldest boy was still trying to decide whether he wanted to be a small ballplayer or a jockey, Myra Cauthen was caring for a cheap mare called Josie's Gal. With more hope than cash at her disposal, she bred the mare to an obscure stallion named Treateat. There were no Derby dreams involved in the transaction. As she and Tex had always done, Myra was just hoping to raise a horse that could run.

Josie's Gal gave birth to a plain-looking little filly. She was named Mary McCullough, in honor of the woman who had helped raise Myra and the other Bischoff kids. Unfortunately, the filly showed no hints that she would gain any more fame than her ancestors. Her speed was limited, her legs unsound. But after two years of solicitous care on the farm in Walton, she made it to the races. Her entrance was through the sport's back door—low-priced claiming races on the Cincinnati circuit—but she brought smiles of satisfaction to her breeder just by becoming a racehorse. And on May 19 Mary McCullough got to play an even more rewarding role in Myra Cauthen's career as a horsewoman. Bred and owned by Myra and trained by Jim Sayler, the filly was to be ridden by Steve.

The race was a stark contract to Steve's victory aboard Red Pipe. Mary McCullough had early speed, and Sayler instructed Steve to use it. She burst out to a clear lead in the opening quarter of the six-furlong race, and Steve did his best to let her save her energy as she led the field around the turn. Then they were in the stretch, which was beginning to look agonizingly long to Steve and to his family in the stands. Like most $2500 claiming horses, Mary McCullough was tiring and feeling her infirmities. Top horses tend to run the final quarter miles of sprint races in 25 seconds or less; the last quarter was to take 27 2/5 seconds for poor Mary. But Steve held her together as she shortened stride, whipping sparingly and nursing her along. Somehow she held on to her lead, and Steve had his second riding victory and his first and best hug from a winning owner. It was hardly a Secretariat performance, but it had a history all its own for the rare woman who had loved and cared for both a winning horse and its rider.

Steve's next victory showed still another dimension of his style. Riding a moderately fast horse named Stallworth, the kid was outrun badly for the lead by a rival, Really Confusion. After a half mile, Really Confusion led by seven lengths. It was another textbook example of when a young rider is likely to panic; a bug boy who has slipped far behind on a speed horse is supposed to hustle him frantically after the leader. But Steve sat still on his mount until he was deep into the stretch. By then the front-runner was staggering—and the kid came on to win by two lengths. Stallworth paid $25.60. And among winning bettors and losing trainers alike, River Downs was alive with conversation about the triple-bug apprentice who had ridden the horse like a patient veteran.

Cauthen won one more race that afternoon and another the following day, and the triple bug was gone from alongside his name. Continuing with a seven-pound allowance, he kept right on winning. At about the time that the Walton-Verona school was concluding classes for the summer, high-school junior Cauthen was becoming the talk of River Downs.

"I know I looked real young, and some people kidded me about it," Steve says. "But I didn't get much needling from the older guys. On the race-track, when people see that you can do something well, there's not much needling about it."

Twelve

"There isn't all that much money to go around at a place like River Downs," says Steve. "Guys aren't racing for headlines, they're racing to put food on the table. So they're fighting for every edge they can get. Some of them, when things get tight in a race, may even think about dropping you. Maybe teach you a lesson or something. A few guys tried that with me, but I never let it bother me. More times than not, you lose when you ride that way."

Food on the table was never a problem for Steve. His father had known his share of hunger in the early years, and paid those dues for the kid. Steve grew up eating heartily: eggs or cereal and toast in the mornings, "almost anything" at evening meals. Even today, while outsiders look at his large hands and feet and speculate about a potential weight problem, Steve eats with verve and enthusiasm. He likes to experiment with seafood and foreign cuisines that never penetrated the Walton scene, and whatever he chooses for dinner, he reaches lustily for bread and orders dessert without a thought. In a profession with rituals that all too often include programmed sweating and induced vomiting, he knows the dual blessing of being able to eat freely—and being able to afford it.

But he also knows the fury that can drive a jockey for whom food or the lack of it becomes a dark obsession. Starving by design in order to stay light enough to ride can leave a man in a foul and angry mood. Starving by not being able to win races can make him desperate. When ill-tempered riders mount horses with physical and mental problems of their own at a place like River Downs, the one-mile racetrack can become a crowded and dangerous place—especially for a teenaged apprentice.

Most modern jockeys ride slightly "acey-deucey": in other words, they lengthen the left stirrup slightly more than the right and ride with the left leg slightly more extended. This is a logical move because it distributes the weight toward the inside rail, helping the rider to lean into the turns as he drives his mount. But in some circles, there is a more subtle reason for "acey-deucey" riding. Jockeys hate to be passed on the inside during a race; if a come-from-behind horse is going to catch them, they at least want to force him to swing outside and lose some ground while doing it. So when an inexperienced jock tries to move up inside a leader, he may find that the extended left leg is also a barricade. The crafty jockey in front will ease his mount over toward the challenger until he can lock his left leg around the rival's right leg and stall his progress.

Patrol films and alert stewards have made the leg-locking art almost obsolete in modern times. But every old pro knows how to do it. Jacinto Vasquez, who learned his trade at his own rough school in

Panama, says, "I always tried to keep my inside iron low enough so that if somebody came up inside me, I could ride my own horse and his at the same time." Vasquez sounds a bit wistful about the technique. "When you take all the trouble to learn tricks like that," he adds, "sometimes you wish that you could still get away with them."

Guillermo Milord, a leading rider at River Downs when Steve was breaking in, shared Vasquez's nostalgia for the old rough-riding days. He liked riding tricks and sometimes he got away with them. But sometimes he didn't. In the first days of Cauthen's riding career, Milord was accused of grabbing the reins from another jock during a race. The stewards examined the patrol films and suspended Milord for 60 days. It was an unusually stiff penalty, and the angry Milord appealed. The state racing commission listened to the complaint and reviewed the films. The suspension was extended to one year. But Milord won a reversal in court, and so he was still around to greet Steve with implacable eyes and to protect the old ways of riding against the upstart kid.

Twice at River Downs, Steve drove his mounts along the rail inside Milord. Twice he found his right leg locked by Milord's left one. After each race, the stewards suspended Milord. But Steve didn't need the stewards to tell him the hazards of sneaking inside Milord on the rail. When he had a choice, he began avoiding such tight spots. And he kept on winning.

These were the lessons that couldn't be learned on bales of hay or in gallops along the backstretch. Even film study can't show a kid when it is wise to aim for a narrow opening between horses—and when the opening has been left only to "sucker" him, so he can commit himself and then be blocked by the veterans in front of him. If

Steve's touch with horses was a matter of instinct, his knowledge of entire races was a more cerebral affair.

"Horses and riders both tend to have patterns," *says Steve. "You can only know them by watching them a lot. Some horses always bear out when they're getting tired, so you can try to move up inside them. Others bear in and close off the rail, so you avoid getting trapped inside them. The same way with riders. Some will let horses drift out when they turn them loose, while others will always be thinking about shutting off the holes behind them. Everybody realizes that a jock should know his own mount. But to really do your job, you should also know all the other horses in a race."*

Jackie Flinchum helped a lot with those lessons. Tex Cauthen thinks that Flinchum may be the finest exercise rider he has ever seen, and Flinchum pitched in because of his admiration for both Tex and his son. But Flinchum saw something more in Steve. He too had known the riding dream once, and it had slipped away from him. Watching the kid at River Downs, Jackie saw it all come to life once more.

Flinchum started riding at 14, in an era when birth records were not too closely scrutinized and a kid on the racetrack could "float his age." He rode well starting in 1939 at Oaklawn Park, and later he moved to Hialeah and enjoyed one sensational winter. But after a few years he was drafted, and in the service during World War II, he grew too heavy to ride. And so to outsiders he became a sad footnote to the Cauthen story: whenever people guessed whether Steve could sustain his brilliance when he was no longer the "hot apprentice," they listed other blazing bug boys who had disappeared, and Jackie Flinchum's name often came up.

But Jackie was not a part of faded history to Steve. He was a man on a constant vigil, warning the kid about things that could go wrong in races: "Watch that front-runner, he'll stop on a dime in front of you and you'll have to pull up . . . Try to be outside that favorite coming off the turn, because he'll lay on you if you're inside him . . . Don't rush up the first time you see an opening in this field. Take your time, they'll come back to you . . ."

"I just told him how to work his way between or around a field of horses," Flinchum says modestly. "I wanted him to get position and use it to his best advantage." But Steve recalls that it was never that simple. Every rider hopes to get position and enjoy clear racing room. It took Flinchum's painstaking analysis of scores of individual races and horses to help Steve become the unusual young jock who consistently avoided traps and traffic jams. "My dad taught me to understand horses," says Steve, "but Jack helped me to handicap whole races." Long after Steve left his seminars with Flinchum, New York horsemen paid frequent tribute to that part of his development. "You watch the kid ride a hundred races," one trainer says, "and you realize that he hasn't gotten blocked a single time. It's uncanny."

To translate the growing backstretch enthusiasm for Steve into "live mounts," Tex Cauthen engaged a popular local jockeys' agent named Eddie Campbell to book Steve's riding assignments. A stocky, wavy-haired man with a ready smile beneath his blond mustache, Campbell was not a high-pressure salesman. Like many top agents, he traded on the friendship and respect of the horsemen. After years in the business, he counted on the fact that trainers would believe him when he said he had a kid who would help for their horses. Campbell also fit well into the Cauthen family's approach to the sport. When he promised Steve's services to a horsemen, he delivered—even when it meant passing up some faster mount that later became available in a race. He wasn't trying to outslick anyone. Like his baby-faced client, he didn't need to.

In the first two months of his River Downs apprenticeship, the kid rode 157 races and won 26 of them. Then the track begin its 56-day summer meeting—Steve's first full meeting as a race rider. With trainers seeking out Campbell for his services, Steve began getting the best horses on a regular basis—and winning at the startling rate. His 96 winners set a record for the meeting, and his total of 120 winners set another standard for a full River Downs season. The hard-riding veteran Carlos Marquez had held the old record of 103 winners. Marquez had set the record in 100 days of racing. Steve topped it, easily, in only 70 days. By late summer, Tex and Steve were thinking about bigger goals. They decided to visit Saratoga.

"I think Steve is ready to take a shot at the big time," Tex told agent Campbell. "At least, he's ready in terms of the racing. But I'm worried about the other things. He's so young, and I don't really know that many people in New York or Chicago. He'll need somebody to guide him. And with all the competition for good mounts, he'll need a good agent."

"If Steve ever gets to New York," said Campbell, "there's only one guy to get. Look for Lenny Goodman."

The advice was a little surprising, because Campbell and Goodman were not close friends. "I used to meet Eddie Campbell maybe once a year, when I went to Kentucky for the Blue Grass Stakes at Keeneland and the Derby," recalls Goodman. "The year before he sent Steve up to see me, I don't remember bumping into him at all. But there was something about the guy that told me that he didn't belong on that leaky-roof circuit around Latonia and River Downs. He always had one of the leading riders around there, and I think he could have moved any place he wanted and done good. But he was happy staying around Cincinnati. And people sure liked him there. He was a bright man and a classy kind of guy." It did not diminish Campbell's brightness or class, in the eyes of the flamboyant and egotistical Goodman, when Campbell told Tex Cauthen that the man to find in New York was Lenny Goodman.

There was still no reason for Tex Cauthen to expect Goodman to leap at the chance to represent Steve. In the volatile currency of jockeys and their agents, Goodman dealt almost solely in pure gold. He had brought Dave Gorman and Bobby Ussery some of their finest triumphs. He had soothed the mercurial Bill Hartark and popularized the gentlemanly Johnny Rotz. For the last 12 years he had represented the icy Panamanian master of pace Braulio Baeza. Goodman's clients had varied in style and temperament, but they shared a common trait. They were established veterans and winners. Big winners. Lenny did not wear cashmere coats, smoke $1.25 cigars, and indulge in a lusty betting habit because he fell for every overnight sensation who rode into New York. In fact, he had not deigned to handle an apprentice rider in 25 years. At many stages of his career Goodman would not have taken on an apprentice even if he had won 1000 races at River Downs or some other outpost in what Lenny scorned as the leaky-roof circuit.

Wandering into the picturesque foreign territory of Saratoga, where agents and horsemen gather under the elms to trade tips about royally bred two-year-olds, the quiet Kentuckian Tex Cauthen made no dramatic announcement about his son. Instead he chatted with a few friends from near home, telling them that Steve had gotten a couple of slow horses to ride that day, just to get the feel of New York racing. Then Tex found himself talking to a young newspaperwoman who was not about to dismiss the Kentucky kid's arrival along with the brief note about it in the daily press handout.

Kay Coyte, the racing writer for the local paper, The *Saratogian*, was just a year out of the University of Kentucky. More important, she was only a year removed from the stable areas of Keeneland and Latonia, where she had gained an unusually deep appreciation of the sport. She had even worked for a Kentucky character named Cadillac Jack Sowards, who had become something of a legend when one of his horses broke loose on the Latonia backstretch, jumped a fence, and jogged right through the door of the track kitchen. Kay Coyte greeted the Kentucky visitors warmly. And the next day, as a 22-year-old working for a small upstate New York paper, she became the first reporter on racing's major-league circuit to warn the public about the kid who would eventually dominate the New York tracks.

"We're looking both here and at Arlington Park in Chicago for an agent for Steve," Tex told Coyte. "Naturally, we've also got to find good arrangements for somebody for Steve to live with. There's no rush, but we hope to work something out." Tex hesitated. "Eddie Campbell suggested Lenny Goodman. But I don't know if he'd be interested in a bug boy. I've also heard some other names, like Ralph Theroux and Joe Schiavone."

Kay nodded. She liked Goodman and knew

that he was the blue-chip dealer among agents. She wondered if Theroux or "Joe Shea" Schiavone might be even more suited to the kid, because both were slightly lower-keyed and more fatherly than Lenny. "If you get any of the guys you mentioned," she said, "you'll be doing fine for Steve. Good luck talking to them."

Tex had no trouble locating Goodman. The agent was standing on the porch outside the racing secretary's office, clenching a cigar in one side of his mouth and discussing an upcoming race out of the other. As he often does, Lenny had an opinion and was preparing to bet that he was right. But when Cauthen introduced himself, Lenny asked a friend to place his bet for him. Then he turned to Tex and listened.

"My son Steve is riding two horses here today," said Tex. "He's the leading rider at River Downs and I was hoping you might look at him and see what you think."

"Tex has something about him that impresses you right away, like Eddie Campbell," Lenny recalls. "I was pleased that Campbell sent him and I liked the way he talked. No big promises. He just knew he had something good." Goodman unfolded his *Racing Form,* studied Steve's mounts for a few minutes, and then turned back to Tex. "These are are terrible horses," he said. "He's got no shot to win. But I'll take a look at him."

What transpired over the next few hours will always remain the subject of some debate. Perhaps more than any other spot in racing, the century-old Saratoga scene is a vantage point for studying the future. Two-year-old racing is emphasized, and horsemen study the young colts and fillies for hints of long-term greatness. Across the street from the track there is an annual high-priced yearling sale, where owners bid large amounts of money, in effect betting that they have predicted future stardom in animals one year old. A few of the projections of Saratoga eventually come true, and horsemen enjoy retelling the stories of guesses that turned out right. Many more midsummer dreams fade into disappointment, and horsemen talk about them too. Mainly, they tend to make excuses for them.

As a result, Saratoga spawns a brand of revisionist history that is a special part of racing. The man who paid $100,000 for a yearling that couldn't run at all came back to console himself with the recollection that he also bid $100,000 for a champion—only to see someone else get him for $110,000. In truth, only a handful of people do any serious bidding on any given yearling. But once that yearling has grown up to be a star, the people who insist that they were underbidders could fill a small stadium. Similarly, bettors who have lost bankrolls backing Saratoga two-year-olds that failed tend to return with an unshakable belief that in between the losers, they once spotted the first workout of a Seattle Slew and made it all worthwhile.

Some observers claim that when Lenny Goodman talks about his first encounter with the Cauthens, he is indulging in a bit of that Saratoga revisionism. They say that when Steve rode his two mounts that day and finished far behind, Lenny watched with only casual interest. They say that if the agent's gaze was suddenly riveted on Steve's balance or the light touch in his hands, he gave no outward sign. They recall Lenny muttering something like "The kid looks good on a horse. But watching him on these bums he rode today, who can tell?"

Goodman denies such suggestions vehemently. "The kid was something special," he says. "Bad horses can't keep a rider from showing that he can ride a horse. The kid showed me plenty." And in the end, Lenny wins the argument. Because whatever he thought or said during the few minutes that Steve was riding that day, he made the right decision. He told Tex Cauthen that he was interested.

Timing had a lot to do with Goodman's decision. If he had been busy at the time with one of his star riders, he would not have had the need or inclination to engage a bug boy, no matter what he saw in him during two losing races. But Lenny wasn't busy in August 1976. His longtime client and friend Baeza was deeply troubled and losing a battle against increasing weight. As incredible as it seemed to everyone who had marveled at Baeza's grace and consistency for more than a decade, Braulio's cold and placid eyes seemed trained at last on the end of a great career. Goodman was troubled by Braulio's misfortunes and he wanted desperately to believe his friend's reassurances that there could still be a comeback. But in practical terms, Goodman was also out of work. It was not a condition that suited his life-style or his reputation. With a feeling of loyalty that is not a standard facet of an agent's repertory, Lenny was determined to stick with Baeza until the last hopes were exhausted. But he also knew that he would soon have to look to the future. If it was blind good luck that the future came to him that day at Saratoga, it only counterbalanced some of the pain and ill fortune that he and Baeza had known.

Baeza's Inca-god countenance presents a sad and striking counterpoint to the eager beardless face of the kid who eventually replaced him with Goodman. Braulio was a great rider and a good man. On and off horseback, he carried himself with dignity and courage that few modern riders could ever match. But as Steve Cauthen turned 16, Baeza was 36, and the emotions and hazards that he had always endured and conquered were finally beginning to break through his imposing demeanor.

The problems first surfaced in the weeks before the Derby that marked Cauthen's sixteenth birthday. Riding Derby favorite Honest Pleasure in the Blue Grass Stakes, Baeza turned in a rare ill-judged performance. When his colt wanted to run freely, Braulio all but wrestled him into submission. Trainer LeRoy Jolley watched in consternation as Honest Pleasure raced down the Keeneland backstretch with his mouth wide open, fighting against the bit as if he were being restrained by some heavy-handed bug boy. Honest Pleasure won anyway, but it was an uninspiring performance by both horse and rider. Jolley was deeply troubled.

"Something's bothering Braulio," Jolley confided at the time. "He's such a private person, maybe we'll never know exactly what it is. But usually he's the smartest rider around, absorbing everything you tell him about a horse. And lately that's changed. You talk to him and you get the feeling he's not listening at all."

In an unorthodox attempt to get his jockey's attention, Jolley refused to confirm Baeza as Honest Pleasure's rider until the last possible moment before the Derby. Braulio was hurt and Goodman was furious, but the team stayed together for the race—and finished second. In the ensuing weeks, however, Baeza grew increasingly remote and evasive. Then, on the day of an important stakes race in New York, he failed to show up to ride one of Jolley's best horses, Optimistic Gal. The race was a showdown between the two top fillies of the season, Optimistic Gal and Dearly Precious. Jolley and Optimistic Gal's owner, Mrs. Bert Firestone, had been anticipating it for almost a year. And in the final minutes before the race, they had to find a replacement rider. Jolley had been roundly criticized for his callous treatment of Baeza before the Derby, but after the Optimistic Gal incident he was uncharacteristically subdued. "I don't want to come down hard on him now," Jolley said. "A lot of people don't know it, but something bigger than any horse race is bothering Braulio right now."

A few days later, people knew. Front page headlines screamed that Mrs. Carmen Baeza had reported to police that her husband was missing. Braulio's quiet, family-oriented life-style had been as well known around the tracks as his reliability. Now he had broken both molds within a matter of days—a subconscious and futile gesture of rage, perhaps, at the weight problem that was ruining the shape of his career. Baeza soon returned, chastened and eager to seek aid. But he has managed only a few comebacks in the saddle. The course that stretches so invitingly now before young Cauthen appears to have run out on the stoic Baeza, who had always tried to measure it off so carefully. Goodman knew what was happening and it influenced him when he looked at Cauthen. But Lenny did not make his move without a tinge of sadness. He would never forget the golden days when Baeza was the hot rider with the game in his hands.

"I like your kid," Goodman told Tex Cauthen that day at Saratoga. "But we got a problem here. He's sixteen. A baby. I can tell him what to do from the time he gets to the barns in the morning until the end of the last race in the afternoon. But when he leaves that racetrack at night, where's he gonna go? I don't want some racetrack hustlers latching on to him and getting him broads and telling him he's the greatest thing since Arcaro. They could ruin him in record time."

"That won't happen," Tex said calmly. "Steve's a levelheaded kid to begin with. And don't worry, he's not going anyplace where he doesn't have someone reliable to live with."

"Well, I don't have any room for him," said Lenny, who had seen enough in two races to take a business chance but not to go into any adoption plans. "Where would I put him?"

"We'll have to find some place sooner or later," said Tex. "But there's no hurry. We'll go on back to River Downs and let him finish the meeting. Then we'll decide if he should try Chicago or New York."

"Fine. When you can work out the arrangements and you want to come to New York, just call me." That will be easy enough, Lenny thought wryly. His phone had not been ringing off the wall with calls from trainers wondering when the absent Baeza would return. He could hardly have guessed that by the time the kid had been in New York a month, trainers and reporters would listen to busy signals for hours every time they tried to get through to the agent with the hot new kid.

"No hustlers were ever going to grab hold of me, then or now," Steve says. "I know that's the first thing people think about on the racetrack. 'A little kid's on his own—watch out for the schemers and the broads.' But I don't go the places where schemy guys go, so I keep them pretty well screened away. And when I go out on a date, I can always find a nice girl my own age, just like any teenaged guy. I just never believed in all those big temptations people said I'd find when I left home to go on the racetrack."

At the end of that happy River Downs summer, the Cauthens chose Chicago for Steve. Jim

Sayler was training some horses there, and he was delighted to have Steve move in with him. Eddie Campbell had a friend, Paul Blair, who was a top agent at Arlington Park. "The way things fell together," says Tex, "Chicago offered the smoothest transition from living at home to living on the road."

The transition seemed so smooth that little was said when Steve prepared to leave Walton. He was departing a home that had always made him feel warm and comfortable, but he was moving in with a man he informally called Uncle Jim—a man who had often told the Cauthens that if he could have a son like Steve, he would want to have a dozen of them. Doug and Kerry joked some about life in the big city for their brother, but nobody in that pleasant farmhouse really believed that the move would change or endanger the kid. It was just another step in an orderly progression that had been ordained for years. It seemed no more wrenching a rite of passage than the shoe-polish ceremony that followed Steve's first winner.

Only Myra Cauthen sensed a more profound meaning. Nightly phone calls and regular visits to Chicago would keep her from missing Steve too much, but she was still conscious that a part of her son's life was coming to a close. Even when he had set his adult goals at the age of 12, Steve had never tried to put childhood behind him. He had continued to laugh and party with his friends and brothers, and he had never taken himself too seriously. Now, as unspoiled as he was, Steve was entering a man's world. Leaving home, perhaps he was leaving childhood for good.

Steve was handling the change so naturally that there was no cause for special sadness. But one night Myra did open the bulging carton of snapshots that had been taken through the 16 years of

131

costume parties and parades and assorted kid stuff, and she allowed herself a few minutes of nostalgia as she fumbled through the pictures. "I never noticed before," she said quietly, "but in every one of these pictures he seems to be laughing or smiling. He must have been a happy kid."

Thirteen

"Did you like Chicago?"

"It was fine."

"What did you do there?"

"Got up in the mornings and worked some horses. I rode in the afternoons. And I went home at night with Jim Sayler and watched television or studied some of my high-school correspondence courses. Then I got up and went to the track again."

"But what did you like most about the city?"

"Riding winners."

In the end, the potentially perilous passage of the country kid to the big city—the passage from the familiar Cincinnati-Walton area to Chicago, from home to the road—became no more than a change in the level of competition. And it held no perils.

Once Arlington Park was a grand name in American racing—a home base for some of the leading stables and riders in the land and a setting for historic events like the 1955 match race in which Arcaro and Nashua defeated Shoemaker and Swaps. But in the 1960s the attractive track in a suburb west of Chicago fell on hard times. Marj Everett, then the controversial owner of Arlington, alienated horsemen by juggling the stakes program on short notice to draw types of horses she favored —creating a "secret stakes" system that drove away more good racing than it created. An experiment with night racing was an abysmal failure. And track management became embroiled in a bribery scandal that sent a governor of Illinois to jail. By the time Everett had departed to take over a much more successful operation at Hollywood Park, California, Illinois racing had descended to a sort of second rank among the country's tracks. Along with Florida the state stands as one of the monuments to what greed and political shortsightedness can do to a once thriving industry.

But for the kid who arrived there in the fall of 1976, Arlington's status was virtually ideal. It was a suitable stepping-stone between the "leaky roofs" around Cincinnati and the fierce top-level competition that lay ahead in New York and California. Cauthen got his chance to handle better horses against better riders than he had faced in Cincinnati. And he took full advantage.

Unlike Goodman, Paul Blair was an agent with a reputation for developing apprentices. Looking back over three decades in his profession, Blair could take pride in the early careers of hot-riding bug boys with names like Lester Wickel, Harold Featherston, and Bryan Fann. After losing their weight allowances, none of Blair's kids had gone on to become household words very far outside their own households, but he remembered them fondly. And now he had a prospect who would make him proudest of all. He was booking mounts for the hottest kid to hit Chicago in years. "I've had some good kids," he told trainers, "but I can't recall a bug boy who ever rode as low on a horse as Steve Cauthen. Watch him—he looks like part of the horse." Trainers watched, and listened, and it became a pleasure for Blair to go to work in the mornings.

Cauthen's 24 percent winning average at River Downs had been impressive, but skeptics could have attributed it to a familiar phenomenon. When a kid gets hot at a small track, he can generate so much excitement among purse-hungry horsemen that he can virtually pick his mounts. Riding the best horses, he naturally wins a high percentage. At larger tracks where there are more good jockeys available, it becomes more difficult for the hot kid's agent to dominate the good mounts—and for the kid to win as much. At a place like Arlington, a winning percentage of 20 would have seemed exceptional. The odds were stacked against anyone soaring much higher.

Blair and Cauthen beat the odds, easily. Steve arrived in the middle of the meeting, when many stables were already committed to other riders on the grounds. But Blair still located a steady flow of "live" mounts, and Steve wasted no time hustling them to the winner's circle. Of 164 races he won 40 for a percentage just a shade below 25. He placed second in the jockey standings to Larry Snyder, the veteran he had studied and admired during many hours of home movies back in Walton. Snyder won 54 races; but he needed 271 mounts to do it.

Near the end of that meeting, a keen observer —or a visionary—could have seen an intersection of the two biggest stories that would later emerge in the sport. The occasion was the Arlington Futurity, the Midwest's richest and most important race

for two-year-olds. In 1976 the event featured Run
Dusty Run and Royal Ski, who would go on to be
prime contenders for the juvenile championship. As
usual, the Futurity attracted horsemen from across
the country, almost all of whom had strong opinions
about horses and riders.

Run Dusty Run beat Royal Ski that day, but
in the clubhouse corners where horsemen gathered, much of the conversation ran to other topics.
"These are nice colts," one Easterner said. "But
there's a colt back in New York who will make
people forget all about these others. Name's Seattle Slew."

"These may not be superhorses here," retorted
a Chicago handicapper named Warren Brubaker.
"But there's a kid rider here who will make people
forget an awful lot of jocks, even in New York.
His name is Steve Cauthen." The discussion is
worth commemorating, because it turned out to be
one of the few racetrack arguments in which both
sides turned out to be dead right. And although
Cauthen wasn't directly involved in the Futurity
result that fall, the race was to prove important to
him. A year later he was to return from New York
to win the Futurity on Sauce Boat—for the richest
victory of his $6 million year.

When the Chicago racing circuit moved across
town to Hawthorne Park, Cauthen endured the first
brief slump of his career. A lesson went with it. At
that stage Steve was a confirmed rail rider. He had
figured out early in the game that a horse racing
along the inside rail travels the shortest distance to
the wire; he had also watched a lot of jocks lose
races because of precious yards that they had sacri-
ficed by swinging too wide. Riding near the rail
demands the patience to wait for openings and the
courage to drive through some tight quarters. It

is a hard style to develop and, in most cases, one to be admired.

But racetrack surfaces are seldom uniform. Soil, weather, and drainage conditions can create a track bias, making it an advantage to be either inside or outside where the footing is best. In the early days of the Hawthorne meet, the bias was extreme: the rail was bad. Young Cauthen, looking for the shortest way home, was traveling in the slowest path.

"I pleaded with Steve," recalls Blair, "but I couldn't get him to take his horses off that rail. He'd enjoyed so much success by waiting for openings down there, he really believed he owned that inside." For a while Steve owned some very undesirable land, and he lost races because of it. But before he could adjust, the track changed in his favor. "Gradually the inside became as fast as the rest of the track," says Blair. "And the kid won all the races."

The rail experience lowered Steve's winning average to a very human 15 percent, but he still managed to place second to Snyder in the Hawthorne, jockey race. And when he left Chicago to rejoin agent Campbell for the Churchill Downs fall meeting, he was a wiser apprentice. "In most cases, I still believe in saving ground on the inside," he says. "But I've learned to adjust when there's a real bias. You've got to take advantage if one part of the racetrack gives you a big edge." By the time he reached New York, Steve seemed able to find the best "paths" on the track with a knack that approached that of the master of bias, Velasquez. But he did not mind a bit when it happened that the best part of the winterized inner track at Aqueduct almost always turned out to be along the inside fence.

The kid's return to Churchill, the scene of his first losing rides, was marked by a fanfare of silence —respectful silence. Horsemen who had scoffed at the kid in the spring sheepishly approached Campbell and asked if he would ride their horses. Because honesty at all costs is not prized as a virtue among crafty hardboots, some Kentuckians claimed that they had spotted the kid's talent from the start.

Track announcer Chic Anderson was more candid. Anderson was calling the races at Churchill at the time; by chance, he would later move to New York at almost the same time that Steve did —and literally shout himself hoarse during some of Steve's multiple-winner afternoons. Recently he was asked if he had known all along that he was watching a star.

"No way," Chic said with a laugh. "In the spring at Churchill Downs, I figured Steve had all he could do just to sit on a horse. One trainer told me he was going to use this bug boy named Cauthen, and I told him, 'You're crazy, all the kid does is hold on.'" The announcer shook his head. "Then Steve came back to Churchill Downs in the fall, and I saw how wrong a guy can be in this business."

Others noticed subtler aspects of the kid's talent. One afternoon at Churchill Steve rode a mare called Luna Moon for trainer Tom W. Kelley. Midway in the race the boy's white riding pants were spattered with blood; Luna Moon was bleeding from her nostrils. Some horses are chronic bleeders, due to internal ailments and weak membranes in the nasal passages; Luna Moon, it turned out, was merely suffering from a bad head cold. But bleeding is a serious matter. Bleeders are barred from racing until the conditions clears up, and a horse that bleeds badly can ruin itself.

As soon as Steve saw the blood, he stood up in the irons and pulled up Luna Moon. Watching through binoculars, trainer Kelley was worried about his mare—but appreciative of the jockey. "Most bug boys would have kept whipping her down to the wire and maybe hurt her real bad," he said. "Steve acted just like an old rider."

Kelley rushed down to meet Cauthen as the kid dismounted. He knew that a bleeder could be upsetting to a jock. But the kid was unruffled. Sounding more like a sympathetic horseman than a bug boy, Steve uttered only one remark. "I'm sorry your mare bled."

"That was it," Kelley marveled later. "He was a pro."

As the fall season wound to a close in Louisville, the Cauthens again had several alternatives. Paul Blair was headed from Chicago to south Florida and would have been delighted to take Steve for a winter campaign at Calder, Gulfstream, and Hialeah. Trainer Chuck Taliaferro, a close family friend who would have taken Steve to live with him, had applied for stalls at Oaklawn Park in Arkansas. And Steve still yearned for New York, especially when veteran Don Brumfield returned to Kentucky after riding in a New York stake and said, "Take a shot up there. I think you'll do real good."

Circumstances made the decision for Steve. Taliaferro didn't get the stalls he wanted in Arkansas and headed for New York; he and his wife Linda would provide an ideal place for Steve to live. Several trainers who used Steve regularly in Kentucky also shipped to Aqueduct, assuring him of a backlog of mounts that he would never really need. Tex Cauthen called Goodman and the agent said, "Send him up here. Let's get started."

Kentuckians sent the kid off with all kinds of

praise and predictions about what he would show New Yorkers. But the best summary of Steve's impact in his home state was probably provided by Lexington turf writer Maryjean Wall. When Cauthen first spoke of New York, Wall shoved all the riding statistics aside and wrote about the things that would be recalled by those who "knew him when": "They will remember a young person who never acquired that rudeness, that cockiness that unfortunately seems to come with every new winner some apprentices ride. They'll remember a young man who was intelligent beyond the average usually found in the jocks' room . . . And they'll remember some other unusual habits, like banking his paycheck each week instead of going off in search of Eldorados or Mark IVs."

"I don't need a big car," Steve says when such thoughts are brought up. "I drive a Cougar. If Farrah Fawcett can sit on it in a commercial, it's good enough for me."

Fourteen

Winter racing in New York is a cold wheel, in every sense of the phrase. It exists mainly for the benefit of state tax collectors and the city's Off-Track Betting parlors. Its reason for being is money, not sport—and it looks the part. Aqueduct at its brightest can be most politely described as functional; warmth was never built into its concrete and steel facades. In winter, when snow is frequent and a freezing wind snaps in off nearby Jamaica Bay, the track can be a bleak and forbidding outpost. Crowds are small by New York standards, and the horseplayers who do show up tend to huddle indoors near the heating system and the mutuel windows. Most of them watch the races on closed-circuit television; they seldom see a horse in the flesh. But if the on-track game seems impersonal, it is positively romantic compared with the spirit in the OTB shops, where horses are taken a step further into anonymity and designated not by names or numbers but by letters of the alphabet.

The best horses flee the winter scene to race in

California or Florida or to freshen up at various southern training centers. But the purse money in New York remains inviting, so there are always enough horses to fill the winter races. There is also a good supply of jockeys—including some of the very best. Riders fight the cold with gloves and ski masks, thermal underwear and Saran wrap in their boots; but they still return from many races with stiff chilled bones and cheeks burned red by the wind. It is a time when even the harshest critics admit that these small athletes earn every cent of the big money they win.

Bowing to economic and political pressures, the New York Racing Association ventured into year-round racing for the first time in the winter of 1976–77. To make the move possible, track superintendent Joe King designed a new one-mile track inside the perimeter of Aqueduct's mile-and-one-eighth main track. "The challenge was to build a track that could survive the freeze-thaw cycles of winter," says King. "To meet it, we used more sand and less clay than on the main track, so it would dry faster. And we added more salt to the base to keep it from freezing. We studied other tracks in the North that have winter racing, but in the end we built one that is unique."

King's inner track is a great success. But like other aspects of Aqueduct, it is a technical triumph rather than an aesthetic one. It is built to endure rather than to soar to heights of thoroughbred grandeur. Its achievement is that it allows the vast money machine of racing to keep churning through all but the worst blizzards. But for those who seek glamour or tradition with their winter sport, the Aqueduct inner track ranks far below those that are framed by the graceful palms of Hialeah or the mountains of Santa Anita—and only a furlong or two above the depressing sterility of an OTB parlor.

But beginning in December 1976, a 16-year-old kid brought the inner track to life. Measuring it off with keen young eyes and stalking it on horseback as if it were his own, Steve Cauthen transformed the track into an unlikely stage for racing's most engaging drama. The darkest of winter days failed to dim the brightness that the kid brought to Aqueduct; cold-weather gloves never interfered with the messages that passed from his hands into the hearts of his mounts. As trainer Phil Johnson put it, "He's a shining light. And boy, does this sport need him now."

Soon the glamor of the Cauthen phenomenon even penetrated the city's green-trimmed OTB shops: people who usually expressed their love for the Sport of Kings in high-sounding words like "Gimme the C horse" began to murmur with regularity, "I want whatever the kid is riding. He's a meal ticket." Steve justified such blind faith with astounding regularity. As his victories piled up, his cherubic face loomed larger than all the numbers and letters that told winter racing's daily stories. Newspapers sent feature writers to the track along with the turf experts, to try to capture the human interest of the country kid who was capturing so much big-city attention. Television and magazine people extended his sudden fame across the country. Steve Cauthen didn't merely spin the cold wheel and watch his numbers come up. He put the numbers in bright lights. He even made the wheel seem warm.

"I'm a percentage guy," Lenny Goodman said from behind the big cigar. "And the racing here is a percentage game. There are a lot of good riders.

You can't expect to kill them all your first time around."

"*I've done good everywhere else and I figure I might as well try the best,*" said Steve. "*If it doesn't work out, I can always go back to Kentucky or Chicago.*"

"*It'll work out. Just don't expect miracles. I figure we can win maybe ten races a week.*"

"*Whatever you say, Mr. Goodman.*"

"*That's right, you do what I say and we'll do fine. And call me Lenny.*"

The kid and his agent were contrasts that could have come out of central casting: the one with his soft old-fashioned caps and soft old-fashioned phrases, the other with the hard edges of speech and style that are part of the agent business and betting on horses and New York itself. But it was only a matter of days before the bond between Cauthen and Goodman was apparent: Lenny was describing Steve's feats with the time-honored jockey agent's pronoun, the first person plurel—"We win another one."

The relationship was based on an affinity of excellence. "You always want the best if you can get it," said Steve. "And I was lucky enough to get Lenny."

"I am the best," said Goodman. "Trainers knew that I hadn't taken on a bug boy in twenty-five years, so they knew I must have come across something special. They knew I wouldn't try to sell them any crap."

Soon the special chemistry of a hot rider and a shrewd agent was taking hold of the Aqueduct scene. Goodman was finding live horses and Cauthen was winning with them. And the more Steve won, the more trainers sought out Goodman. The agent's projection worked out. In three weeks in December, the kid won 29 races.

But the numbers intrude. They define the scope of what Cauthen was doing in New York, but they miss the emotions he inspired. Numbers can't cry out like the gleeful winners who called him Stevie Wonder, or the losers who frequently were Cauthenized. They can't cheer, and they can't even boo like the fans who naively believed that he could somehow win every race—and then moaned after his losses, "The damn kid is setting us up—he'll break us yet." To appreciate Cauthen's entrance into New York, you have to listen to those sounds and savor their moments.

Pat Lynch, a veteran handicapper and track executive, was watching a race from the Aqueduct press box. Cauthen was riding the favorite, Buttonwood Lane. Going down the backstretch, Buttonwood Lane was third, in what appeared to be a perfect position. Then, with a half mile to go, the other six jockeys in the race began to ask their mounts for speed. Cauthen remained motionless. And his horse dropped back to last.

"Either this kid is making a fool of himself," said Lynch, *"or we're watching the coolest young rider since Shoemaker."*

In the stretch, Steve seemed to answer the question. Finally he cocked his whip. He hit Buttonwood Lane righthanded and the horse began to accelerate. Then he passed the whip to his left hand and hit his mount again, three times. Buttonwood Lane surged past most of the field, then swerved toward another horse. With no exaggerated motion, Steve gathered up the reins and straightened his horse. He won going away.

"I've got to see this again to believe it," said Lynch. He watched a videotape replay intently, and came away muttering his admiration. Like Doc, the chartist who was burned by Cauthen on Monsi, Lynch is a serious handicapper. He wagers according to speed figures that have been refined over a lifetime, not because of momentary adulation of jockeys. But now he found himself getting into a habit of reviewing Cauthen's rides.

"The kid is a genuine throwback," Lynch concluded. "Modern tracks are hard and fast, and the premium today is on speed. The Latin riders, in particular, are always trying to use their horses' speed to get the jump on their fields. Everything in riding today is go-go-go. Nobody wants to sacrifice position in a race just to save a horse for the finish. It's too risky. It can make them look bad when it doesn't work. The only one cool enough to do that consistently is Shoemaker." Lynch shook his head in amazement. "And now this kid. This sixteen-year-old kid."

When such comments were reported back to Walton, Tex Cauthen wasn't amazed at all. "Most horses can only go all out for a quarter mile or less anyway," he said. "It makes sense to have them doing their all-out running at the finish. That's something Steve and I talked about quite a bit." Tex smiled. After a lifetime around horses, he loved the fact that under his son, horses were finally doing things that made sense.

"Some horses pull themselves up when they open up a clear lead," trainer Phil Johnson was saying. "But this filly is special. She'll pull herself up even before she gets to the front. She'll use any excuse to stop trying near the finish. You almost have to trick her into winning."

The Kid

"Yes, sir," said the kid. "I know what you mean."

The filly's name was Ms. Vitriolic. And Steve Cauthen tricked her.

The need for such tricks stems from one of the intriguing ironies of racing: Humans can spend generations trying to breed and train a racehorse that will be competitive, only to have that competitive instinct turn against them. Some horses inherit competitive spirit in the genes, and exhibit it the first few times they are turned out in pastures to romp with the other weanlings and yearlings of their age group. Others must be taught during months of early training. Still others may not deign to dig their feet into a track and try to beat their rivals until they reach the races. And some, sadly, never acquire any fighting spirit at all.

But even among those who learn well and give freely of themselves, there is a hazard of arrested development. Even a very talented animal may absorb the message that he is supposed to catch all the horses in front of him on the track—only to pull himself up once he is in front, assuming that his task is completed. This tendency can turn winning efforts into heartbreaking defeats, and it is a major cause of nervous tension among the canniest of veteran trainers. It is also a major challenge to the teenaged rider who would overcome it.

Several truly great horses have displayed this habit. Native Dancer never saw much point in exerting himself once the opposition had been disposed of, and his regular jockey Eric Guerin had to measure off the big gray's stretch drives with precision. Sometimes the Dancer's overwhelming superiority would carry him to comfortable victories in spite of himself. But he could also turn easy triumphs into tantalizing narrow escapes. His trainer Bill Winfrey still recalls the 1954 Metropolitan Handicap, in which the Dancer threw in a smashing stretch run to catch the good campaigner Straight Face just a few strides before the wire. Years afterward, Winfrey still marveled over the photograph of that finish. It shows Native Dancer in front by a neck. But it also reveals that in the few seconds between the completion of his assigned task—the overtaking of Straight Face—and the official end of the race, Native Dancer had pricked his ears and lost all interest in the proceedings.

Buckpasser was an even more flagrant and fascinating case. Perhaps more than any horse of modern times, the big, almost perfectly conformed bay colt symbolized the narrow line between the perfectibility and the fragility of the thoroughbred. And so when a racetracker confronts a startling, seemingly magical new talent—horse or man or teenager—it is hard to resist recollections of Buckpasser, the horse that did so much and just missed doing much more, the horse that might have stood atop some mythical scale, measuring off the natural countervailing forces of ability and luck that shape racing's dreams and its nightmares.

Bred by Ogden Phipps, a giant of the sport, Buckpasser had the credentials to be a giant in his own right. His sire was Tom Fool, a Horse of the Year. His dam, Busanda, was a great race mare and a daughter of Triple Crown winner War Admiral; Busanda was also a direct descendant of perhaps the most influential broodmare of the 20th century in America, La Troienne. Describing Buckpasser's bloodlines, the astute and generally understated commentator Kent Hollingsworth once wrote, "The riches get so embarrassing here, there is reluctance to mention Man o'War in this pedigree."

The bloodlines rippled to life in Buckpasser's flesh. He was not a breathtaking presence, a "living flame" on the order of his contemporary Dr. Fager or the later champion Secretariat. His beauty was more subtle, often demanding an insider's knowledge before it could be appreciated. But it was there: Dr. Manuel Gilman, who has inspected horses on New York tracks for more than three decades, once commented that while most horses have a hundred faults, Buckpasser was built without a flaw.

Better yet, he could run. As a juvenile champion, he set a record for earnings by a two-year-old. Later he reeled off 15 victories in a row despite carrying high weights against good competition. He retired with earnings of almost $1.5 million and strode quickly into the Hall of Fame.

But again the numbers intrude. They are a mere footnote to the excitement that the colt inspired, not with his bankroll or even with his near-perfect body, but with his quirky, competitive mind. Buckpasser loved to run at horses and catch them, but saw no point at all in running on his own. He hated morning workouts, and his trainers, Bill Winfrey and the late Eddie Neloy, had to employ teams of workmates to encourage Buckpasser to extend himself at all. In his races, he ran just fast enough to get his job done. Of his 25 career victories, more than half were by margins of less than a length. In the richest victory of his two-year-old campaign, he squandered almost all of an easy four-length lead before winning the Arlington-Washington Futurity. In his best race at the age of four, he reversed the script, spotting the good horse Ring Twice 22 pounds and a seemingly insurmountable lead before nailing him at the wire in the Suburban Handicap.

But the drama that will most certainly outlive

Buckpasser occurred near the start of his three-year-old season at Hialeah. It was to be a year of mixed emotions for the people around Buckpasser; a hoof injury kept him out of the Triple Crown races, and he had to charge through a brilliant late campaign to assert himself as the champion. But the race that crystallized his worst and greatest moments within a few seconds was the 1966 Flamingo.

That was the infamous Chicken Flamingo. Hialeah management, shortsighted and obviously unfamiliar with Buckpasser's flair for the dramatic, became so sure that he would win the Flamingo that betting was canceled on the race. The angry public reaction to that cowardly move started a downward spiral from which Hialeah is still struggling to recover. But amid the furor, Buckpasser transformed a sour spectacle into a stage for a feat that is still cherished even by the bitterest of audiences—horseplayers denied the chance to bet.

Braulio Baeza, Buckpasser's regular rider, was a student of the colt's whims; he usually timed his winning rallies so cleverly that Buckpasser never had a chance to pull himself up. But Baeza was under contract to ride another great colt, Graustark, that winter. So trainer Neloy sent for Shoemaker, who promptly proved that no rider is immune to the guile of a headstrong thoroughbred. On the final turn of the Flamingo, Buckpasser was striding so powerfully that he virtually dragged Shoemaker to the lead. Like the misguided track officials, both Shoemaker and the fans assumed that the colt would continue to a wide-open victory.

But once he reached the front, Buckpasser fooled everyone. He almost seemed to prop his front feet into the ground to apply the brakes. By the eighth pole he had relaxed completely and surrendered the lead to a game little colt from the wrong side of the thoroughbred tracks—an Illinois-bred named Abe's Hope. With Kentuckian Earlie Fires whipping him furiously, Abe's Hope opened an astonishing two-length advantage over the favorite. The mighty Buckpasser was a beaten horse.

Then, only a few strides before the wire, Buckpasser caught sight of Abe's Hope. As if to make up for his earlier laziness, he all but hurled himself through the air. His acceleration defied belief at that moment, and it still defies description. Perhaps the best analogy to what Buckpasser did is a human one: he looked almost like a sprinter thrusting and diving desperately for the tape in an Olympic dash. And somehow he made it. He won by a nose.

It was a performance that could only humble those who think they understand racehorses. Jockey Fires, robbed of what had seemed the sweetest victory of his life, sat in the jockeys' room and wept unashamedly. Nearby, Shoemaker was subdued, and more than a little amazed. Shoe said that Buckpasser had responded to late lefthanded whipping. But neither he nor anyone who watched could shake the feeling that Buckpasser had responded to some quality that cannot be touched by the whips or plans of humans. He had won his finest race the same way he had almost lost it—with a willful, competitive mind of his own.

For every Buckpasser, of course, there are hundreds of horses with similar habits but far less ability; they know how to lose races but not how to win them. New York horseplayers still laugh when they think of some animals that kept coming close through years of campaigning and still managed somehow to avoid appearances in the winner's circle. One such horse was Ecuador II, who closed so resolutely without ever getting up in time to win that fans insisted that his tombstone should be inscribed with the final call of all his races: ". . . and that's Ecuador II, coming on." Then there was Dr. Nadler, a horse that finished second and third so often that some gullible souls always bet on him— despite the fact that he remained a maiden for more than 30 races. On the occasion of one antiwar march during the Vietnam years, some young Aqueduct regulars printed pamphlets announcing an organization called Horseplayers for Peace. They dedicated the movement to Dr. Nadler, "the only horse in training which will always accept a nego- tiated settlement at the eighth pole." More recently there was Monsi, apparently destined for life as an also-run—until Steve Cauthen hit New York.

Steve never saw Buckpasser, but by the time he reached Aqueduct he knew all about horses that didn't want to win races by wide margins. The bad horses at River Downs had prepared him well for mounts like Monsi—or the recalcitrant Ms. Vi- triolic. The kid wasn't bragging when he told train- er Johnson that he knew what he meant about Ms. Vitriolic. He was stating a fact, in the same calm flat way he had once spoken to his father: he was ready.

"I'm not a jockey fan," said Johnson. "I don't believe it when people rave about them, and I don't pay much attention to what they say about horses. But before I ever met Cauthen, I'd been down in Kentucky and I'd heard some of those tough old hardboots, guys who would claim that Secretariat was just another nice horse, and they were really impressed with the kid. So I knew he was something special." Johnson paused as he re- called that December day. "Still, I didn't get too optimistic about Ms. Vitriolic," he added. "I didn't care how confident Steve sounded. I knew he'd have his hands full with this filly."

With a sixteenth of a mile remaining in the

race, Steve's hands were very full. Ms. Vitriolic was pulling hard at the bit, charging into contention on the outside. To her cheering supporters, she looked like a winner. But Phil Johnson knew that she had looked that way before—only to pull herself up when she reached the front. She was still a maiden, and if she had her own say, she would remain one. Amid the cheers, Johnson was unmoved, expecting the worst.

"Then I saw something I couldn't believe," said the trainer. "Any other rider might have rushed the filly to the lead at that point. It would be a natural reaction, and you couldn't even blame the jock. But the kid was different. The wire was approaching, and he wasn't moving a muscle. He waited and then he waited some more. And at the last possible second, he got onto her. She made the lead right at the wire, and before she could pull herself up, she was a winner. Steve really did trick her."

Ms. Vitriolic did not bear the trick gracefully. A sixteenth of a mile past the finish line, as if to show her resentment, she dug her toes into the track, propped herself straight into the air—and threw Cauthen to the ground. Steve lay on the frozen track for a moment, then picked himself up and walked back toward the winner's circle. Johnson rushed down to greet him and to apologize for the filly's misbehavior."

"I'm OK," said Steve. "I'm just glad she didn't decide to do that sooner."

Months later, Steve happened to ride Ms. Vitriolic again. He had ridden a hundred-odd winners in the interim; the filly had raced a dozen more times without winning again. "I remember her habit," Steve told Johnson with a smile. "I'll be ready for her this time." Johnson was surprised at the kid's memory. But he was less surprised at the result. Steve never gave Ms. Vitriolic a chance to prop, before or after the finish line. And he tricked her into winning again.

By the time the Aqueduct meeting was adjourned for a brief Christmas holiday the kid's feats were the talk of New York. When a newspaperman was assigned to do a story on how jockeys planned to spend their vacations, he naturally approached the sensational apprentice. Other riders had told of their plans to relax at sunny resorts or otherwise celebrate the end of a hard campaign. Steve said that he was looking forward to going home to snowy Walton and spending Christmas with his family.

"After all you've done here," the writer chided, "don't you think you could spend a more exciting holiday than that?"

"What," asked Steve, "could be more exciting than that?"

Fifteen

"Where's all the cash, Steve?" demanded eight-year-old Kerry Cauthen. "I'm ready to go downtown and start tearing through that money of yours."

In the warm farmhouse living room with the Christmas tree in one corner, the Cauthen family laughed at the youngest member. Steve's mounts had won $1,244,423 during his eight-month campaign in 1976. His 10 percent share, minus agent Goodman's commission and other expenses, amounted to more money than anyone had ever assembled at the south end of Main Street. But it did not provide any sudden infusion into the economy of downtown Walton.

"We're just putting the money in the bank," said Tex Cauthen. "There's not really that much to make us think about any fancy investments, anyway. And money can't change the way you look at things. I mean, Steve's making more than I ever did. But then his income could all come to an end tomorrow."

Tex spoke with a racetracker's fatalism. He was well aware that Steve's career was still measured in weeks and months, not in the years of endurance and excellence that had underscored the greatness of men like Arcaro and Shoemaker and Baeza. Then there were Steve's large hands and size-six boots, inescapable hints that the skinny frame might fill out and the kid might someday outgrow the dream that he was living. Taking stock of Steve's first year as a race rider, Tex Cauthen liked what he saw. But both father and son understood that racetrack people were still watching with a certain skepticism. Even words of praise for the young apprentice tended to end in question marks. Nobody was ready to take Steve's future for granted. Least of all on South Main Street.

Myra Cauthen was taking stock in a different way that Christmas. "Kerry will always be Kerry, the family comedian," she said. "But Doug is so close to Steve's age, and he knows he's getting too big to enjoy the same career, so I worried a little about how Steve's success might effect him." Then Myra's face lit up in that shy, proud smile that often comes when she talks about her sons. "I shouldn't have bothered, I guess."

"I don't think there's any reason to be jealous," explained Doug, who was 13 at the time. "It might be different it we were both football players and Steve proved he was tougher than me. But I can't get mad just because I'm growing faster than he is. And by watching how hard Steve's worked for what he wants, I figure I'll be inspired to try to be the best at whatever I do in my life."

Myra also worried about Steve—but not very much. "He's always had a way of taking things in stride," she said. "On one level, I thought I should be nervous about him being on his own in New York. But deep down, I knew he could handle the responsibility. He's a levelheaded kid. He adjusts."

As it turned out, the adjustments in Steve's routine in New York were minimal. Chuck and Linda Taliaferro offered him a temporary home that was remarkably like the one he had always known. The Taliaferros were not only close friends who shared the Cauthens' love of horses, but they were also young, attractive people who approached life with the same clear-eyed, understated humor that Steve had learned in Walton. Even his education was not drastically altered. Instead of paging through textbooks at Walton-Verona while dreaming of riding in races, Steve was using some non-riding time to peruse correspondence course lessons from the University of Eastern Kentucky. In both classroom and correspondence courses, Steve admitted, American history often finished a bad second to biographies of great jockeys—and Steve's deepest thinking was reserved for probing the psyches of thoroughbreds. But he was making the effort, and his parents were satisfied.

"Like most mothers, I guess I'm kind of an idealist about the kids," says Myra Cauthen. "I always hoped that they would grow up to do something for mankind. When Steve started making all this money and getting so much attention, I wondered a little if it might mess up the real values in life for him or Doug and Kerry. Then I saw him on TV once, and he was saying, 'Excellence in anything is admired, so I want to be a good example for a lot of people.' So by the time he came home from New York that first time, I figured he was handling everything just fine."

Christmas was quite, the New Year an explosion.

When Steve returned to Aqueduct, it seemed

as if every trainer in New York had spent the holiday reviewing his statistics—or more likely, closing their eyes and recalling that smooth, "grinding" finishing style that had won for them or beaten them enough times to leave an indelible impression. Certainly, as Steve and his father and agent had foreseen, the canniest horsemen still harbored their doubts about the kid. They would wait and see how he survived his loss of the five-pound weight allowance, his first serious accident, his first whirl with women and the nightlife. But those events were in the distant future; racing is a "now" business, and the immediate fact of life at Aqueduct was that a 16-year-old was riding and thinking like 30. The hot apprentice owned the frozen inner track, and sharp trainers rushed to share a piece of it with him.

What happened next was that Steve Cauthen changed the rules of the game. The accumulated lessons of December—the lessons of Monsi and Frampton Delight, Illiterate and Ms. Vitriolic—had their telling effect on trainers, bettors, and other riders. There was rarely a race in which agent Goodman did not have a pleasant choice between several "live" mounts. As trainers began to wait in line to get the services of the kid, Goodman started to revise his ten-victories-per-week projection. Then he forgot all about it. There were no numbers that could put a limit on the phenomenon.

Steve's presence soon skewed the entire betting pattern of New York, and turned it into a perplexing riddle. On the one hand, people bet so religiously on him—particularly on OTB parlors—that his mounts never offered any "value" to shrewd horseplayers. With Cauthen aboard, a legitimate 10–1 shot might become a weak 4–1 chance, and a horse worth perhaps 4–1 would become a "false favorite" at 8–5. But again and again, Steve made the false favorites come true. One newspaper kept a running chart on how a bettor would be doing if he made a $2 win wager on everything Cauthen rode. Astonishingly, despite the badly deflated prices on his horses and the inexorable 18 percent that is taken out of every wager before anyone gets paid, Steve kept his imaginary followers in the black for two giddy months. Every serious horseplayer knows that even the greatest jockey cannot make a bad horse win. But among the students of the sport who were continually burned by the kid, Steve seemed to be winning with an awful lot of horses that could be described as mediocre at best.

The jockeys' room scene also changed dramatically. Camera crews and reporters tracked every step of Steve's daily journeys from snack bar to ping-pong table to shower. Among the veterans who watched the action were Angel Cordero, who held the money-winning record that Steve was to break that year, and Jorge Velasquez, whose record of 299 victories in a New York season would fall to Cauthen by August. Cordero is Puerto Rican, Velasquez Panamanian. Both had to battle their way through small, rough tracks in their homelands and then overcome a language barrier in the U.S. before reaching the top of the game. And neither had ever been surrounded by the media as Cauthen was. They were entitled to some resentment toward the white teenager who was getting it all so quickly.

"But who could resent a kid like Stevie?" asked Cordero. "He's such a good kid, you can't yell even when he beats you."

"He respects people and pays attention," said Velasquez. "And he learns fast."

"The rest of us," laughed Cordero, "we're just glad Stevie doesn't ride every race, every day. At least he leaves a few for the rest of us to win."

There were days and weeks when Angel's exaggerated joke seemed very close to the mark. Three years earlier, Cordero had set a New York record by winning 22 races in a six-day racing week. Cauthen dawdled for exactly one week of 1977 before taking aim at that mark. Beginning on January 10, Steve rode an amazing total of 13 winners in four days. Then he accelerated. He won 5 on Friday and 5 more on Saturday—including a stakes race on his old friend Illiterate, the filly who had been his first New York winner. His ride on Illiterate was a classic example of the kid at his best. For most of the six furlongs of the Interborough Handicap, Steve appeared to be trapped along the rail. But instead of bulling his way to the outside for racing room, he waited. Finally a narrow hole opened along the rail in front of him. He drove Illiterate through to victory.

"I was lucky to find room on the inside," said Steve. "And I was lucky that the mare ran through the opening with such courage." In the case of rider as well as horse, courage and brains seemed to have more to do with it than luck. When he returned an hour later to win the week's final race, Steve had a total of 23 victories—believed to be a record week not only for New York but for the whole country.

The following Saturday Cauthen played a variation on his record-breaking theme: six winners in one afternoon, tying one of the most prestigious records in New York. The winners followed a pattern that was almost eerie. All were heavily bet, and four were favorites despite somewhat limited credentials. Steve allowed each horse to settle into stride and drop off the pace, often along the rail where they would lose little ground on the tight turns of the inner track. And each overtook the leaders with that steady rhythmic acceleration that

left the front-runners—and those who bet on them
—"Cauthenized."

By the time his final winner, a horse called
Turn to Gin, had crossed the wire in the near dark-
ness of the ninth race, Cauthen had reached new
stardom in New York. On the local Saturday television show, he was full of smiles and gratitude toward trainers as he was interviewed. There was no
false modesty, no pretending that it was just another day. He cheerfully admitted that he had
known about the record and was delighted to get
it—particularly since the cheering crowd had included his father.

But Steve had to cut short the interviews in the
jockeys' room. He was rushing to join Goodman on
the evening flight to Los Angeles, where he would
make his West Coast debut the next day at Santa
Anita. He had ridden all nine races on the Aqueduct card. He had not finished out of the money
once.

"Are you tired?"

*"Not when I ride six winners," said Steve. "I
only get tired when I ride losers."*

*Cauthen was booked to ride four horses at
Santa Anita, then fly back with his agent on the
"red-eye," the night flight that leaves Los Angeles
at 10:45 p.m. and arrives at Kennedy International
Airport at dawn on Monday. "Will the kid be
rested enough to ride again Monday at Aqueduct?"
someone pressed Goodman.*

*Lenny rolled his big cigar around in his mouth.
"This kid?" he said. "Are you kidding?"*

California presented a stark contrast to winter
racing in New York. Cauthen and Goodman left
wind-chill factor of —35 in New York and emerged

into bright sunlight at Santa Anita. For the first time in months, Steve had no need for his surgical gloves or the Saran Wrap in his boots. But changes in equipment didn't change the magic. His presence brought Santa Anita its largest crowd of the winter. Track officials estimated that of the 42,506 people on hand, perhaps 10,000 had been drawn by the kid. And one thing was certain: they bet on him as if they had all spent the winter watching him in New York.

Cauthen's impact was extraordinary. California racing is set off from the rest of the industry by money as well as geography. The purse structure is so generous that many horses and riders establish headquarters in the state and leave only for championship races in the East. So California is a wheel unto itself, and many visitors find it less than hospitable. From Citation to Seattle Slew, modern eastern champions have often ventured into the West only to encounter unexpected defeat. Eastern riders have had just as much difficulty breaking into a talented local riding colony that features Shoemaker, Laffit Pincay, Jr., and many other top reinsmen, most recently including young Darrel McHargue. Californians are justifiably proud of the local talent and hesitant about accepting newcomers. But by the time the kid had flown in, ridden for a day, and arrived back at Aqueduct, at least one Los Angeles headline had proclaimed: CAUTHEN CAPTURES L.A.

Steve's first day in the West started inauspiciously. His first three mounts were heavily backed by the public, but the best he could manage was one third-place finish. Then the fans seemed to regain their California perspective. Steve's mount in the second division of the San Fernando Stakes, Elmendorf's Pocket Park, was dismissed at odds of

21–1. Pocket Park had won only 2 of 24 starts prior to the race. He hardly seemed to belong with the favored Cojak, ridden by Shoemaker, or the local hero Crystal Water, who had Pincay in the irons.

Trainer Ron McAnally instructed Cauthen to take a good hold on Pocket Park and make one late run at the leaders. The well-laid plans remained intact for only a few strides. "I was trying to take him back," explained Steve, "but he ran off with me." To his consternation, the kid found himself much closer to the leaders than he had hoped. But he adjusted immediately, and somehow convinced his overanxious mount to relax and remain just off the pace. In the stretch, he was third. Pincay had Crystal Water battling for the lead along the rail; Tony Diaz and Properantes were on the outside. Cauthen decided to drive Pocket Park between them.

It was the kind of chilly move that had been setting records from River Downs to Aqueduct. But at Santa Anita it almost resulted in disaster. Just as Pocket Park entered the hole between the horses, Properantes swerved to the inside and cut him off. Cauthen had to stand up in the reins and check his horse sharply. He lost perhaps a length —and apparently, the race. But then he dropped back down over Pocket Park's neck and got him going again. Keen observers gasped at the kid's poise in the face of near catastrophe. The rally fell short and Properantes prevailed by a neck. But the stewards immediately flashed the inquiry sign: minutes later, Properantes was disqualified and Cauthen had his first California victory.

From the unruly start through the stretch incident, it hardly ranked as one of Steve's prettiest performances. But it won $38,600 for Elmendorf owner Max Gluck—and thousands of new admirers for the kid. Professor Gordon Jones of the *Los Angeles Herald Examiner*, a handicapper whose credentials in skepticism are solid, called it "a gutsy display of saddle artistry." More poetically, Robert Hebert wrote in *The Blood-Horse* magazine, "He seems to fit a horse as snugly as a dove's wing."

The Santa Anita jockeys' room, a home to champions who know their own stature, sounded like an instant fan club. "The kid is just too much," said Canadian star Sandy Hawley, an Eclipse Award winner. "It's hard to think of him as a sixteen-year-old." Shoemaker, after posing cheerfully with Cauthen for the inevitable publicity shots of the old and new champs, said quietly: "He thinks well, sits nicely, and he has that gift of making horses run better for him. He's very, very good and he can get even better." Later, 69-year-old John Longden, who set all the winning records that Shoemaker eventually broke, and also retired to train the Kentucky Derby winner Majestic Prince, added a final note from the West. "Every now and then in every sport, a natural comes along," said the leathery Longden. "You can see that this kid was born to it."

"I'll be back next Sunday," the kid told listeners in California. "And I hope I'll be here a lot of other Sundays. The only difference will be that next time, I'd like to ride in all nine races. That's what I'm here for—to ride horses."

That was the point that some outsiders kept missing. As Steve's incredible run of success continued on both coasts and at points in between, people kept asking about the physical toll it was taking on that deceptively slim young body. They didn't understand that riding was the easy part of it all. Spare time was also a joy, whether Steve was relaxing in the Taliaferros' Elmont, Long Island, home, talking to his parents on the phone—or even turning away from television or racing books to delve into eastern Kentucky's history and English programs. The kid found himself able to handle every aspect of his fast-paced life—except the people who kept asking him about it.

"I guess that reporters come in different levels of class, just like horses," says Steve. "Some of them show that they understand the business and they respect your privacy and your need to concentrate. But others keep pushing at you with their questions or cameras until you want to burst. I mean, you want to yell at them to just leave you alone. But of course, you don't want to get folks mad or sound like a spoiled kid. So you keep it inside you and it can drive you crazy."

Finally Goodman and Chuck Taliaferro did some discreet yelling for the kid. After consulting with clerk of scales Jim Zimmerman, the man in charge of the Aqueduct jockeys' quarters, they announced that Cauthen would be available for interviews before each day's races but not in between them. A jockey who competes in all nine races in a day, as Steve usually does, gets only about ten minutes between races to change silks, wash up, weigh in, and think about his business; Steve and his advisers decided to claim those intervals as private ones. "Steve understands that the reporters have a job to do," said Goodman. "But he's entitled to time to do his job, too. A lot of these guys, they don't leave him a chance to breathe."

"Steve appreciates the good press he's been getting," Taliaferro added soothingly. "But we had to do something to help him concentrate and avoid fatigue. People have to remember that this is not a grown, mature man." But people could be forgiven for forgetting that point, too, as they watched Steve's performances. On the day that his no-interview rule went into effect, for example, Steve quietly went out and swept the last four races on the Aqueduct card—including still another stakes victory.

As he settled into a calmer routine—if seven-day weeks, transcontinental commuting, and breaking almost all records in a man's sport can be called a routine for a teenager—Cauthen found time for some of the laughter that should go along with his kind of career.

For anyone who hopes to discern whether the kid's talents are more mental than physical, his jockeys' room recreation may be instructive. At racehorse rummy, a game of skill and nerve, he quickly became one of the big winners. At ping-pong, a test of quick reflexes, he is eager but no more than adequate. Steve approaches the ping-pong table like Muhammad Ali, jumping on his toes, issuing challenges, and predicting victories. But when a visitor examines the fine print of the draws for jockey ping-pong tournaments, Cauthen's name can usually be found in the second flight. Many of his matches end with shouts of anguish and the paddles thrown to the floor in mock disgust. While he claims to be improving steadily, he still needs all the "apprentice allowance" or handicap points he can get when he faces better players like the local champ Velasquez.

But even his fun and games may be revealing. Steve can't beat Velasquez at ping-pong or Jacinto Vasquez at checkers. But at cards, he can handle even the craftiest older valets in the Aqueduct room. And racehorse rummy is where the most money is won.

For sheer silliness, no incident in his career matched Cauthen's brief encounter with the bureaucrats of New York State's Department of Labor. Steve was already working on his second hundred victories in New York when some vigilant clerk apparently noticed one of the scores of articles or TV shows about him—and decided that he had cleverly spotted a teenager who was making money without the working papers required by law. In a state where teenaged unemployment at the poverty level is a pressing, potentially explosive problem, the Labor Department quickly trained its sights on the affair of a Kentuckian who was making about $2500 a day—and doing a very poor job of hiding his crime, out there in front of about 10,000 people each afternoon.

"This is a criminal statute," a Labor spokesman intoned with a straight face. "Our job is to enforce the law." Horseplayers found this technicality very amusing—much funnier, for instance, than other bureaucratic inspirations like the uniquely regressive withholding tax that is slapped only on small bettors who win a lot while betting a little. But Cauthen, innocent in the ways of government, wasn't laughing. Neither were the incredulous trainers who learned that they could be fined or even jailed for the crime of employing the kid.

The threat triggered the sort of paper chase that warms the bureaucratic heart. Tex Cauthen rushed from Walton to the Kentucky state capital in Frankfort to obtain documents certifying Steve's age and valid jockey's license. Then he drove to Cincinnati and sent the papers by courier to New York. They arrived on a Friday night, but since state offices were closed for the weekend, they could not be processed. This gave state investigators a chance to visit Aqueduct on Saturday and warn darkly of the penalties they would inflict when they caught up to the owners and trainers who were riding Cauthen. Fortunately, the conspiratorial denizens of the track did not alert the sleuths to the fact that the names of owners and trainers were listed alongside their horses in secret documents like the daily program and the *Racing Form*. So no arrests were made, the technicality was cleared up on a Monday morning—and the manhunt was called off.

"You know," said Jan Nerud, one of the horsemen involved, "there are a lot of sixteen-year-olds working for less than a minimum wage because they have to eat. Wouldn't you think these Department of Labor guys would be out trying to help them?"

"Ridiculous," snorted offended taxpayer Lenny Goodman.

"I still don't understand," Steve Cauthen said quietly, "what all this commotion has been about."

Other interludes were more pleasant. On their California trips, Cauthen and Goodman dined in Beverly Hills spots like Matteo's and the Bistro, where the kid shook hands with movie stars he had once watched at the Florence Drive-in—and realized only gradually that they were as thrilled as he was about the introductions. He also met Irving (Swifty) Lazar, a literary and show business agent whose clients have included Hemingway and Bogart, Cole Porter and Richard Nixon. Poised somewhere between putting together the blockbuster TV series "Rich Man, Poor Man" and selling the ex-president's memoirs, Lazar was not exactly hungering for new clients. But he was a horse owner and a horseplayer, a jockey-sized man with a vast sense of the excitement of Steve's career. Lazar spoke of vast advertising contracts, movie deals, and this book. Lenny Goodman listened carefully.

"Irving is the best, right?" said Lenny, who

ends many sentences with questions that do not call for answers. "Well, the kid's had nothing but the best so far, so why stop now?" The kid had himself another agent. The celebrity kind.

There were other memorable times in New York, the best of which probably came when Myra Cauthen made her first visit to Aqueduct, accompanied by her brother Tommy Bischoff. Myra picked a good day. Chuck Taliaferro won two races, with Steve riding one of the winners. "We wanted him to ride both of them," Linda Taliaferro explained, "but in one of the races, Lenny had Steve booked on another mount."

"It doesn't matter," Steve said calmly. "I ride what my agent picks for me. If he misses a winner here or there, he usually makes up for it pretty quick."

Later, Myra and Linda waited for Steve outside the jockeys' room. Jorge Velasquez spotted Linda, who is slightly younger and blonder than Myra, and thought it was Mrs. Cauthen. "Hey Steve," he said, "your mother looks young enough to be your sister."

Then Myra was pointed out to Velasquez. "Hey Steve," he said, "your mother still looks young enough to be your sister."

Steve took his mother and uncle and the Taliaferros to see the Broadway hit *Chorus Line*. Then they went to Sardi's, where they received appropriate celebrity treatment. "I hadn't been to New York in about twenty years," recalls Myra. "Steve really made it a treat. I had worried that he would look a little tired from the schedule he was on, but he was as full of life as ever. We all had a lot of laughs."

The day after his dinner party at Sardi's, Steve was kidded about picking up the $200 tab for the *evening. "Normally," someone said, "sixteen-year-olds don't pick up checks like that."*

"Normally," he answered, "sixteen-year-olds don't have enough money."

If the living was good, the riding was better. The records came in bunches throughout the winter. One day Pat Lynch looked out from the Aqueduct press box toward the frozen infield lake and said, "I'm waiting for the ice to melt, to see if the kid can walk on water." The kid didn't try, but he did keep up his winning pace even when bigger stables with better horses arrived for the spring.

"You watch any rider long enough," said Aqueduct steward Bud Hyland, "and sooner or later you expect to spot some weakness. But we watch this kid nine times a day, and we haven't seen that weakness yet."

Then, to the delight of those who sought assurance of his mortality, Steve revealed his weakness. Singing. Under the guidance of enterpreneur and horse owner Alan Rosoff, for whom Steve won many races, the kid recorded an album, *And Steve Cauthen Sings, Too*. Rendering a series of hokey country lyrics about such musical milestones as winning the Derby, the kid gave it his usual sincere effort. But the result can be best summarized by the fact that the most favorable review was offered by the artist's mother. "It wasn't for real music lovers or Frank Sinatra fans," says Myra, laughing. "But we thought it was kind of fun."

Classic magazine, a handsome bimonthly that is a kind of repository of the highest traditions of all forms of horsemanship, disagreed sharply. In the only other notable review of the album, *Classic* lamented over the crass commercialization of racing and warned that someday Steve would look back and regret his role in producing such "crow-bait." Actually, Steve foresees little occasion for remorse in the future, because the record's musical qualities were well matched by its distribution. For better or worse, hardly anyone heard it.

Sometimes, watching the kid as he autographed records for giggling girls in a Manhattan department store or listened to the business projections of Swifty Lazar in Beverly Hills, it was hard to remember the one astonishing fact about him: he had left the farm and the bales of hay and the 4-H club ponies only a year before. He had started as a country kid with all the doubts and hopes that go along with a wild dream, and now he was not only celebrity and teen idol; he had put most of the doubts behind him. The big meals at the fancy restaurants hadn't added an ounce to his frame, and if his weight was ever to become a problem, it seemed a faraway one. He was sought after to ride in stakes races, without benefit of his five-pound allowance, and he was winning them frequently. So most horsemen had long since ceased worrying that Steve would flop when he lost his "bug." That left only one possible stumbling block—the one that could never be predicted, prepared for or measured off in ounces or pounds or yards of track.

Eddie Arcaro was among the first and loudest to bring up the subject of serious injury. The master of an earlier generation, Arcaro is entitled to feel proprietary about his own era—and in 1977 he became an increasingly curmudgeonly guardian of old-timers' perspectives. During the Triple Crown races he carried on a running feud with the owners of Seattle Slew. When Eddie dared to mention that Slew's times and the level of competition may not have established the colt as the rightful heir to Citation or Secretariat, Slew's fans rose up in protest. Arcaro's strident remarks on television were no less unseemly just because they happened to be true.

On the subject of jockeys, and particularly of the young star of the season, Arcaro was equally brusque. Both Eddie and his friend and heir apparent Shoemaker had paid for their riding records with several long stints in hospitals. Just because young Cauthen was breaking some of those records was no reason for Arcaro to confer greatness on the kid until he had also logged his hospital time. "Let's not put him on a pedestal yet," warned Arcaro. "If he rides long enough, he's going to have spills, and you never know how he will react. Some riders can't take the physical shocks." At the slightest urging, Eddie went farther. "Don't start telling me how great a jock is," he snapped, "until he's broken his collarbone about five times."

"I don't think about spills," said Steve. "I've been falling on my head since I was a little kid."

"When I hear about a bad spill someplace, I worry that it might happen to Steve," said Myra. "I worry, but not too often."

Tex Cauthen expressed even less concern. "I know what Steve will do if he gets hurt," he said. "If you've got true heart, there are plenty of ways to show it. And Steve's shown me."

Sixteen

"The horse snapped a leg. I remember going down, and then the horse going over the top of me. And that was all."

That was all. The kid's helmeted head smashed into the grass of the Belmont Park turf course, and he lost consciousness. There was never a split second when he could have paused and thought, "This is it. I've been lucky so far but now it is going to happen to me." The horse simply broke a leg, and it registered in Cauthen's mind the way any other bit of data might have registered. "Horse is bearing out. Horse is tiring. Horse snapped a leg." It was just another lesson, another experience. And it was over very quickly. It was left to the ambulance attendants and trackside observers and doctors to piece together what had happened to the kid. And then it would be up to the kid to show everybody what it might mean.

The date was May 23, 1977. It was among the strangest days of racing in New York history, and

173

it was to provide a stark and ominous setting for a bad racing accident. If Steve's rise to the top of racing had elements of a fairy tale, his jolting fall seemed part of a dark and barely understood absurdist drama.

It was opening day at Belmont Park, a day that annually offers leafy new surroundings and bright promises to horseplayers who have endured the winter and early spring at steel-plated Aqueduct. This time it had a special attraction: the seasonal debut of the huge, gallant Horse of the Year Forego. And then there was the new challenge that Belmont presented to the game's young riding star, just turned 17. The unchallenged king of the tight turns of the one-mile inner track at Aqueduct, Steve had adjusted effortlessly to the wider mile-and-one-eighth main course at Aqueduct. Now he was ready to try the biggest racetrack in America, with its mile-and-one-half circumference and sweeping turns—and all the subtle switches in strategy that they would require.

Steve had done his homework. He knew that hugging the rail would be less important on this new track, and the timing of his stretch drives would take on even more importance; he was anxious to take on the challenge. He was also interested in seeing Forego, which would be ridden by Shoemaker. The stretch-running gelding had already been Horse of the Year three times. But Steve had only seen him perform on television. This was understandable, since the Rider of the Year was only ten years older than his equine counterpart.

But Steve was not to see Forego this day, and those who believe in omens and superstitions around racehorses might have anticipated that fact. From the beginning, this Belmont opening was all wrong. The mutuel clerks, the people who sell the tickets and cash the winning ones, were on strike. There was no betting at Belmont. The track was open for the sole purpose of giving Off-Track Betting customers something to bet on. More than 7000 fans showed up anyway, lured by free admission and the presence of Forego; this total was perhaps 7000 above what might have been expected by cynics who assume that horseplayers who can't bet don't care about watching good horses. But somehow, in the absence of the low steady whirring sound of the mutuel machines—the sound that is a siren call to the hard-core players known as mutuel ticket junkies—the track seemed very quiet and empty.

Cauthen's mount in the fourth race was a solid stretch runner called Bay Streak. "He warmed up just fine and for most of the race he ran just fine," said Steve. Coming out of the final turn on the grass course, Bay Streak was moving smoothly on the outside. There were no narrow holes to probe through, no apparent problems. He looked like a winner. Then the leg snapped.

Earlie Fires, the Kentucky rider whose path has crossed young Cauthen's at several points, once described the feeling of riding a horse that breaks down: "It's like he comes to a staircase that he doesn't know is there. Suddenly he steps off that top step and bam!" Others have likened the experience to having a horse plunge suddenly into a deep hole. "I didn't have a chance to think of what if felt like," said Steve. "I just felt him stumble badly, and I reached down on the reins to try to help him up, and then I knew that I just couldn't help this one."

In a second, horse and rider were down. The canny Velasquez, just behind them on a horse named Volney, had no time to pull out of the way. Volney and Jorge plowed into Bay Streak and

Cauthen and also went down. A third horse, Low Return, also crashed into the group, but jockey Pat Day was able to leap free of the carnage and the horse galloped away unhurt.

As it often does, the fiberglass helmet that jockeys are required to wear under their bright silk caps undoubtedly saved Cauthen from a serious head injury. But the rest of him was vulnerable. In the tangle of horses, he was hit about the face and ribs and arms. Velasquez got it in the head and ankle. Like Bay Streak, Volney broke a leg; both horses were destroyed moments later.

The first men to reach Cauthen were struck by the blood. His left eye was puffed and closed and the blood was pouring from a slash over the eye and another across his nose; his right hand was also bleeding badly. But behind the blood and bruises they saw that beardless baby face, and some of them forgot all about the year of record-breaking race riding that the kid had put in. All they could see was his youth. "It was," said patrol judge Jack O'Hara, "like seeing one of your own children lying there."

Velasquez and Cauthen were rushed to Long Island Jewish Hospital. Jorge was found to have a broken ankle and a concussion. Steve had a broken bone in his right arm just above the wrist, a fractured rib, two broken fingers, and a severe concussion. The cut above the eye needed ten stitches. The slash on his arm required fifteen.

The kid awoke with Linda Taliaferro standing over him. "The doctors say you'll be OK," she said. "How do you feel?"

Steve paused and blinked a few times, taking stock of himself. "The rib hurts the most," he said. "And the rest of me, well, I'm still trying to figure out just what happened."

*Later, as he recuperated back in Walton, the
kid was asked about those first moments after he
opened his eyes in the hospital. Was it like coming
out of a nightmare? Was there a flash of fear?*

*"It was confusing for a little while," he said.
"But not scary."*

Perhaps Steve's attitude was youthful and
naive. Perhaps it even smacked of hubris. He was
17 and sitting in his living room with a cast on his
wrist, and he had not even had the chance to show
that his heart and psyche would be unaffected by
his fall. Yet he was viewing the whole affair with
the same clear-eyed placidity that he once brought
to the first spotted pony he ever mounted, to Slade
in Lonnie Abshire's barn, to the first rogue animals that jolted him off their backs around Latonia. There was no arrogance intended. But an
outsider had reason to wonder if the kid might be
taking a rash chance, tempting the bad racing luck
that had interrupted and even destroyed other
great riding careers.

Certainly the older masters had been more
willing to admit caution, even fear. Arcaro, the man
who had raised the injury issue long before Cauthen's spill, once said, "There were plenty of times
when I was afraid. Every day something would
come up that would give me a scare. But I figure
when I signed my name to be a jockey, death might
be a part of it."

Arcaro suffered many spills during his brilliant
three-decade career. But fate reserved the worst
for near the very end. Eddie was 43 when he rode
Black Hills in the 1959 Belmont Stakes. Near the
end of the final turn Black Hills was moving up
along the inside. Then he went down, pitching Arcaro head first onto the sloppy track. Walter Blum

on Lake Erie, just behind Black Hills, tumbled into him. Blum also went down. But as Blum struggled to his feet, Arcaro lay motionless, face down in the mud. Observers called it the most terrifying accident they had ever seen. Arcaro's father, watching from the stands, thought his son was dead.

Arcaro regained consciousness in the ambulance, with pain shooting through his neck and upper back. The injury turned out to be less serious than it looked or felt; he had suffered a severely bruised neck. But some observers felt that the experience would be enough to encourage the greatest rider of the century—a man who needed no more fame or money—to retire. "You'd have to put a gun to my head to make me stop riding now," Arcaro replied. And so he made a comeback, and rode for several more years. He was willing to acknowledge fear. But he still had to show that he could conquer it.

Shoemaker was also a veteran when he encountered his worst spill. He still has a vivid memory of watching an apprentice rider create a dangerous jam in front of him, yelling to the kid to watch out—and then plunging helplessly into the pileup that the boy had created. Shoemaker's mount in that 1968 race at Santa Anita, Bel Bush, kicked the rider after they both fell. It broke the femur bone in Shoe's right leg.

The injury sidelined Shoemaker for more than a year. He turned 37 during his convalescence, and like Arcaro, he had accumulated enough records and cash to allow him to retire. It could have been an easy choice, because the enforced idleness caused Shoemaker's leg muscles to deteriorate and his knees to stiffen. A comeback demanded hours of arduous and boring physical therapy, But Shoe endured, and on the day of his return he won three races. Then he went home and cried with joy.

Other stories lack the happy endings. The most poignant of our time involves Tony DeSpirito, the kid who won 390 races back in 1952 and virtually owned the New England racing circuit—including its women and its big cars. Tony's license said that he was 17 during that year, but it turned out that he had lied. He was 16. The Steve Cauthen of his time.

Then the spills began. DeSpirito said he knew no fear, and perhaps that was his undoing. Perhaps he suffered from too much courage, too much confidence that he could take chances and get away with them. In a series of accidents, he broke his back, his ribs, and his jaw. He was trampled by one horse, dragged along the track by another. He lost his spleen and a kidney. Pain became a constant in his life, and when the medications failed to erase it, he tried to deaden it with the Scotch and the nightlife. Again and again the pain made him quit, but he kept trying to come back as his money and his talents slipped away from him. He was planning still another comeback in 1975 when he died. The autopsy determined that, perhaps in some final rebellion by all the parts of his body that had been broken and worn out and abused, he had choked to death. Tony DeSpirito was 39.

So warnings are in order, and the masters are quick to provide them. "It takes most riders a little while to put a spill out of their minds," Shoemaker says in his autobiography. "You're bound to think about it. Sometimes you're edgy for a while. Most guys are—those that have any common sense, that is."

"You develop a wonderful feeling of control over horses when you're riding successfully," retired champ Ted Atkinson once said. "But I never realized how big horses could be until I was down —lying spilled on the track. Then every one that comes up over you looks as big as a house. I'll tell you this," Atkinson added ominously, "it's easier to want to forget a spill than it is to do it."

A headline in a New York paper trumpeted the news with flair. STEVIE'S MOTHER: "HE'LL RIDE AGAIN."

Actually, there was no dramatic family council about the matter. There was no need. Injury was a matter of concern to Tex and Myra Cauthen. But it was not a source of shock. Like Steve, they had known it would happen at some point. It was part of a bargain that had been struck long ago, when Steve decided to get serious about the bales of hay in the loft, maybe even when Tex first ventured out of Texas and took up the racetrack life in New Orleans. Even when Myra flew to New York and gasped at the first look at the ugly bruises on her son's face, Steve's not riding again was no more viable an alternative than his not breathing again.

Myra had been talking long distance to a friend in New Orleans when the news reached her in Walton. An operator cut in and said it was an emergency, and for a split second Myra held her breath. Then she heard Linda Taliaferro shouting into the phone, "He's all right. Don't worry. He's all right." So even before she had to cope with the details of Steve's injuries or the marks on his face, there was reassurance. There was more reassurance from the doctors, and then from the calm strong voice of the kid himself. By the time she faced reporters in New York, Myra was speaking in the measured tones of a woman who knew racing almost as well as she knew her son.

"This won't revise our plans about his future," she said. *"He wants to race. And we're going to let him."*

There is a scene in one of Francis Ford Coppola's *Godfather* movies in which a character based on underworld czar Meyer Lansky arrives at Miami International Airport. As he walks down the airport concourse, the Lansky figure is surrounded by reporters with notebooks and cameras and probing microphones, all snapping questions toward him like a pack of mechanically armed small dogs, all hoping for some unlikely scoop or hint about secrets that the man has guarded for a lifetime. Amid the chatter, the Lansky figure strides coolly and untouched, saying little and revealing anothing.

In the era of electronic media overkill, perhaps it was not all that surprising that the Lansky scene should have come to mind on the afternoon when a 17-year-old race rider left Long Island Jewish Hospital. Steve had spent two days in the hospital, chatting amiably with nurses and other patients, watching television and reading the *Racing Form*. His broken wrist was set, and doctors were satisfied that he had recovered from his concussion. His mother was pleased that his spirits were high. As he prepared to go home, he could have been any one of the kids in rooms filled with flowers in the hospital's adolescent unit. Then he emerged into his public world.

As Steve rode his wheelchair into the hospital lobby, more than a dozen photographers and television cameramen turned on lights and elbowed for position. Both of the kid's eyes were black and swollen and partly closed. Instinctively he raised his right arm, with its cast and sling, to shield his face. But the radio people bore in, brandishing their tape recorders and thrusting microphones at the small bruised face. "What happened?" the voices kept demanding, in search of some secret fears or epiphanies. But Steve had no mysteries to unravel for them. "Horse snapped a leg," he repeated patiently. Then Myra Cauthen and some security guards eased him through the crowd and into a "getaway car," and Linda Taliaferro drove him home.

Steve remained on Long Island for several days at the Taliaferro home, then went back to Walton. Little had changed. A few old high-school friends came around, and Steve joined them to go to movies or just hang out for a while. But many local kids were too shy to look up the kid who had become a star. And the kid seldom bothered to call them. He was not, as some of them might have expected, a spoiled brat who thought he had grown too important for them. He just happened to feel comfortable around his own house, studying and reading, watching television and talking to his parents about riding. "It's not that I don't want to see other kids," he explained. "It's just that from the time I decided what I wanted to do, the people I enjoyed being around the most were racetrack people."

"I think this injury may have been a blessing in disguise," Myra said at one point. "The way Steve was going, riding seven days a week and doing all that traveling, he might have gotten worn out before the year was over. This way, he can come back and get a fresh start."

"Maybe this rest will help me in the long run," admitted Steve. "But right now, all I know is that I'm itching to start riding again."

Others were just as eager for his return. Racetrackers always want quick answers; if they had more patience about finding out what was happening, they would presumably invest their money in stocks or real estate or something else that doesn't tell you what your return is after six furlongs in a minute and 12 seconds. Now that the riding phenomenon of his generation had been forced to the sidelines and confronted with the new challenge of coming back, a lot of people were anxious to see how he would react. It was a little like waiting for the ice to melt on the infield pond. Would the kid walk on water this time?

The timing of the accident added to the tension. Cauthen had been scheduled to lose his apprentice allowance on May 27—four days after the spill. Like all bug boys in similar circumstances, he was granted an extension because of the injury; his apprenticeship would now last four days after he returned to the saddle. But after that brief acclimatization, Steve would be forced to cope with two major tests at the same time. By themselves, the injury and the loss of the bug would have each presented certain problems. But when fate made them happen almost simultaneously, the sum of their impact threatened to become greater than the individual parts.

No one in the jockeys' room understood this cumulative threat better than veteran Mike Venezia. Fifteen years older than Cauthen, Venezia is a respected journeyman now. He is popular with fans, horsemen, and the colleagues who have made him president of the New York chapter of the Jockeys Guild, and he has no difficulty in making a good living from his profession. But Mike remembers when it all figured to be much easier for him —almost as easy as it looked for Steve Cauthen when he was about to lose his bug. Venezia also recalls how hard it suddenly became, and how long it took him to climb out of the wreckage that followed the loss of his bug.

Like Cauthen more than a decade later,

Venezia had once been a record-setting apprentice. It seemed inconceivable that horsemen would desert him just because his horses would be required to carry an extra five pounds. But the loss of the bug triggered a series of disasters for him. First he took out a kind of insurance policy by signing as the contract rider for the Greentree Stable. This assured him of some mounts on the prestigious Greentree horses, but it also required him to show up at the Greentree barn in the mornings to exercise horses. This meant that he could no longer free-lance around the Belmont and Aqueduct stables, galloping horses for trainers who might later give him mounts in the afternoon. An eager youngster who had built his career largely on hard work and hustle, Mike had unwittingly signed away his freedom to do his hustling.

Worse yet, just as his apprentice allowance expired, Venezia drew a suspension for careless riding. When he returned, he was suspended again. Then he contracted tonsillitis. At the very moment when he most desperately needed to ride and prove himself without the bug, Mike lost more than a month. He learned that many racetrack memories do not endure that long.

Venezia returned with his skills and enthusiasm intact. But he returned to some trainers as a stranger. New apprentices were already grabbing attention with their weight allowances and victories. Older riders had taken over some of Mike's steady mounts. On the basis of no evidence except his prolonged absence, some horsemen had decided that Venezia was no longer valuable without the bug. And without live horses to ride, Mike was unable to jog the critics memories or prove them wrong. Trapped in that vicious circle, he languished in a prolonged slump. In the long run, he showed the strength of character to come back.

But his hard-won success only underscores the fact that in racing, hardly anything turns out as easy as it seems.

"I guess I was a little like Steve," says Venezia. "I tried to handle success in a levelheaded way, but I was still young and impressionable. I couldn't really believe that everything could turn so bad in such a hurry. But losing the bug and getting those suspensions just about finished me off. I think the worst thing about it was the feeling that it was all beyond my control. Something like that makes you pretty humble, because it forces you to realize that some of the success was beyond your control, too."

Cauthen completed his convalescence in Key Largo, Florida. Tommy Kelly, a trainer who had also become a good friend, loaned the Cauthens his Florida home. Steve fished and swam and counted the days until his return. Then he went up to Belmont and spent two mornings galloping horses, making sure he was ready. He knew that men like Kelly would suffer no memory lapses about his talents. Other regular clients seemed just as glad to have him back around the barns. But he also knew that horsemen's memories would include the sight of Bay Streak crashing to the turf with him. He would have to prove very quickly that he had put the accident behind him. And it had been no ordinary accident. "You'll only see a worse one," said veteran trainer Johnny Nerud, "when you see somebody get killed."

"I know the trainers will be watching me," *Steve said as he prepared for his comeback ride.* *"But that won't bother me. They'll see the same things they saw before."*

The horse's name was Little Miracle. Like so many of the stage props around the kid's real-life story, it could have been a playwright's inspiration. Sometimes it seems that the elements of romance in racing are aligned in some vague conspiracy against the kid who would prefer to take things in his laconic stride. Steve wanted his first ride after his injury to be a routine success, not a symbol. He would have been perfectly satisfied to return aboard some mundanely named beast like Queen Boor or Uncle Ugly. Lenny Goodman, who does not support his expensive tastes by picking mounts with pretty names, would have put the kid on anything that could run. But by coincidence, rider and agent got more than they planned on. They got Little Miracle.

A crowd of journalists trailed Cauthen as he walked into the saddling area on June 23. The fans around the walking ring cheered him and yelled their welcomes. Steve grinned and tipped his cap, and the cheering increased. Alan Marcus, the trainer of Little Miracle, shook the kid's hand and then gave his simple instructions: "Get a good position and then go when you're ready."

Cauthen followed the orders perfectly, placing Little Miracle along the rail behind the leaders. Turning into the stretch he was third, with dead aim on the two leaders, Nose for Nose and Pilot's Son. At that point he could have swung to the outside. Instead he chose to drive up between the front-runners. The opening was narrow, and for a moment it appeared that Steve might be blocked. But his instinct for such openings had not been dulled at all during his month away; and those who had wanted to see his nerve and guts in tight quarters got a very swift answer. The leaders allowed him just enough room, and he drove Little Miracle smoothly to the lead. "That's Little Miracle AND Steve Cauthen in front," yelled announcer Chic Anderson. The crowd responded, and the

kid coasted through the roar to a comfortable victory. It was his 277th of the year, and one of his
most significant.

The winner's circle was every bit as crowded
as it had been two weeks before when Seattle
Slew had won the Belmont Stakes and the Triple
Crown. "How does it feel?" the microphone hold-
ers kept yelling.

"Just like it always has," said Steve. "Good."

"I wasn't worried about using him after the
layoff," said trainer Marcus. "And of course I'll
keep using him after he loses the bug. He follows
instructions, gets the most out of his mounts, and
generates class and poise."

"He's a freak," exulted another regular client,
young trainer Nick Zito. "He's Joe Namath, Muhammad Ali, and Carlton Fisk all rolled into one."

"Carlton Fisk?" someone asked.

"That's a rich compliment," said Zito. "I'm a
Red Sox fan."

In his floating office on the second floor of the
Belmont clubhouse, Goodman was approached by
other trainers. Their words were less hyperbolic,
but the message was always the same. At a critical
juncture in the kid's career, horsemen were no
longer withholding judgment. They were getting
in line to use him.

Three days and five winners later, Cauthen
rode for the first time without the bug. "Today,"
someone told him in the jocks' room, "you become
an official jockey."

"I was an official jockey," he said with a smile,
"the first time I got on a horse."

His first mount as a journeyman was a filly
called Hutchinson Gal. Steve had won twice with
her back at Aqueduct during the winter, and she
should have been an old friend. But she wasn't
feeling friendly at Belmont. As she entered the

gate she tried to toss Steve off her back. When that failed, she simply sat down in the gate and refused to move. Finally Steve dismounted, and Hutchinson Gal was scratched. With his keen sense of the ill luck that can accompany such occasions, Mike Venezia said, "I hope for Steve's sake that this isn't an omen."

It wasn't. The kid picked himself up and won the next three races. "There are some kids who need the weight allowance," said Phil Johnson, who trained one of those winners. "You might like them, but you just know that you'll have to drop them when they lose the bug. But Steve isn't one of those kids."

Then Johnson recalled a story, possibly slightly apocryphal, about one of those unfortunate kids: A bug boy was once riding regularly for the late Hirsch Jacobs, perhaps the most successful trainer of all time. At one point the kid won six straight races on a Jacobs horse. Then, on the morning when he was supposed to go for a seventh victory, Jacobs asked casually, "Say, don't you lose your bug today?"

"Yes, sir," said the kid. That afternoon, Jacobs put Arcaro on the horse.

Johnson chuckled as he told the tale, and the laughter seemed infectious among those who cared about Steve Cauthen. Injury and apprenticeship were behind him now. The two big tests had been passed. "Tell all the people who've been wondering," said Goodman, "that the kid and I won't have to look for a new line of work for a while."

In the swarm of media people who attended the Little Miracle race, the kid had sometimes appeared strangely vulnerable. His skinny body looked as if it might be overwhelmed in the crush; his expression was quizzical, as if he honestly wondered what all the fuss was about. Then two cameramen, jostling for position in the walking ring, began shouting at one another. Cursing, they almost came to blows. Steve watched them and allowed himself a smile. His reaction could have summed up his feelings about the injury, the apprentice allowance, the people who doubted or didn't understand him—even his approach to riding racehorses.

"Be patient," the kid said quietly. "It's a virtue."

Seventeen

"I've never had a trainer yell at me."

That statement may be as close as Steve Cauthen ever comes to bragging. In the business of winning horse races, trainers and jockeys are uneasy partners. Horsemen live with the constant awareness that while a jockey may need only ten minutes to warm a horse up and another minute and a few seconds to get him from starting gate to finish line, the same horse may have required countless hours of care and preparation before he was able even to walk onto the track. This ratio of time spent does not delight most horsemen—or encourage them to divide the glory of victory on an equal basis with the rider. As Cauthen's friend Tommy J. Kelly puts it, "When everything goes right with a horse, the rider can be the icing on the cake. But you never forget that you can point six months of labor toward one race and watch a rider screw it up in a few seconds."

As wary as they are about sharing honors and

compliments with jockeys, horsemen are much freer with blame. This tendency is not a result of any special meanness, but of the delicate position of most trainers, who are balanced between their thoroughbreds and the people who own them and pay the bills for feeding and handling them. The successful trainer must be able to train his owners as well as his animals. If he cannot offer enough explanations, attentions, and results to keep an owner satisfied, his horsemanship will be wasted because the owner will take the horses elsewhere. A lot of grooms, exercise riders, and assorted race-track hustlers once failed as trainers because they could virtually talk to horses—but never could talk soothingly enough to their owners. Conversely, more than a few successful trainers are clever enough to hire skilled foremen to supervise their stables while they concentrate on beguiling wealthy spenders.

The jockey plays an important role in this system. When a trainer predicts to an owner that a horse will run well, and it doesn't happen, the trainer will seldom confess, "I was wrong. I didn't have him fit enough. I made a mistake." For purposes of job security it is much easier to insist that the jockey "moved him too early," or "got the poor horse blocked just when he was getting into high gear," or otherwise ruined the well-laid plans. One racing axiom holds that there are a million ways to lose a race. Certainly there are a million excuses for losing. And from the trainer's point of view, the jockey figures in the majority of them.

At Pimlico Racecourse in Baltimore, a humorist once decorated the bulletin board in the racing secretary's office with a list called "The Trainer's Manual of Excuses." The list included many standard complaints of riding ineptitude, as well as more exotic laments: "This little filly just didn't like that mud kicked back in her face . . . That colt was just beginning to make his move when he shied at a piece of paper that blew onto the track." The trainers who came into the office laughed at the list. But not too loudly. Almost everyone recognized some excuse that he had used himself on some owner.

One landmark in excuse history occurred some years ago when veteran trainer Jimmy Pitt shipped a promising filly from Atlantic City to Aqueduct for a stakes race. Ridden by Barry Pearl, the filly broke slowly from the gate and trailed the field all the way. Pearl dismounted with a rare explanation: "The bell that rings when the gate opens is louder in Atlantic City than it is here. The filly never heard this soft bell, so she didn't break."

"You've just made it worth the trip up here," said Pitt. "I've blamed bad starts on a lot of things. But now we can have owners worrying about whether their horses are hearing bells."

New York jockey Oswaldo Rosado recalls a more macabre incident. In their quest for ready excuses, many trainers seek out tiny idiosyncrasies in a horse's behavior during a race, then tell owners, "I can't understand it. This horse never did *that* before." Once Rosado was working a horse at the little Finger Lakes track in upstate New York when the old animal suddenly collapsed in a heap on the track. The trainer ran onto the track, barely glanced at the rider who lay crumpled on the ground, and then stood over the horse. "He's dropped dead," he said. Then he turned to Rosado out of habit. "I can't understand it," he said, "He never did *that* before."

Finally, there is a classic tale of the beleaguered trainer who once gave detailed instructions to the great Arcaro. "I want you to get position about fifth," he said. "Then move up grad-

ually on the outside, and try to be laying third
when you turn for home. Then start hitting him lefthanded and make your drive to the wire on the
outside."

The horse broke slowly and ran with thorough disinterest to finish last. The trainer gestured
furiously to Arcaro as he returned to dismount. "I
thought I told you to move up . . ." he began.

"What?" said Arcaro. "And leave the horse?"

For every gag line, of course, there are a hundred defeats that produce no smiles at all. Horsemen function under a pressure as relentless as
any in sports. Even great horses create enormous
tension. No trainer has ever developed a Derby
candidate without thinking of colts like Gen. Duke
and Sir Gaylord, heavy favorites that broke down
only hours before the call to the post at Churchill
Downs. Thousands of fans learned the perils of
training a star when they cried over the fatal injury
that befell the magnificent filly Ruffian in a match
race at Belmont; but many more disappointments
occur in quieter settings, when trainers arrive at
barns in early morning to be warned by sad-eyed
grooms that a season's hard-earned profits are about
to turn to losses. "Better check the big horse, boss.
Something's wrong."

Cheaper horses generate a different brand of
pressure—but it is no less real. When a trainer
claims horses out of races and in turn loses horses
that are claimed by others, he is constantly betting
that his opinions of horses' values will be a little
sharper than those of his rivals. If he bets wrongly
too often, he loses not only races and horses, but
his owners and livelihood. Buddy Jacobson once
summed up the unique strain of the claiming competition as well as anyone: "Where else does a guy
have to put his entire business up for sale in order
to make a profit on it?" Understandably, the situa-

tion jangles nerves and raises voices. So it is not an insignificant fact that no trainer yells at Steve Cauthen.

Trainers come in many shapes and styles, with various techniques of handling the common pressure. Among Cauthen's major clients, for example, Tommy Kelly is a warm fatherly man who has virtually welcomed the kid as a family member; Frank (Pancho) Martin, king of the claiming business, is gruff and profane and noisily confident that he can accomplish anything, as long as some rider doesn't mess things up. Lazaro Barrera is courtly and debonair, while Nick Zito is young, brash, and cocky. Phil Johnson is practical about his chances and wry about his setbacks, but rotund Johnny Campo tends to be overly optimistic about his prospects, jubilant in his many victories, and explosive in defeat. Agent Goodman needs a range of psychological ploys to keep them all happy, particularly when Cauthen is unavailable to ride for them in certain races; in times of crisis, Lenny also makes good use of a thick skin. "But that's not my problem," Steve says with a grin. "That's what a good agent is for. He's got to keep them satisfied in the mornings. Then I can just worry about keeping them happy in the afternoons."

The kid was sitting in the back seat of a car borrowed from the Pinkerton security agency, alongside trainer Tommy Kelly. Cauthen had just completed a day's work at Saratoga, and now he was headed for Atlantic City to ride a horse in a nighttime stakes race for trainer Kelly. The Pinkertons had agreed to rush the trainer and his jockey from the beautiful Saratoga track to nearby Ballston Spa airport, where a private plane awaited them. On a back road, the car passed two kids standing alongside bicycles. They were being questioned by a state policeman.

"Wonder what they did," Steve said. "Looks like trouble for them."

"They look about your age," he was told.

"Could be. I didn't get that good a look at them." Then the kid was talking horses again. The contrasts were striking: between his Pinkerton escort and the routine police run-ins of other teenagers, between private planes and bicycles and between a "doubleheader" racing schedule and the idle routines of other kids on this warm August evening. But the contrasts slipped right past Steve, and it was left to Kelly to remark on them. "I think it's as if you gave violins to a thousand kids," Tommy said later on the plane. "You can give them all the same encouragement, maybe even the same lessons. And only one ends up making beautiful music." The trainer smiled broadly. "We're lucky to be around that one of a kind."

That evening Cauthen had roughly the same effect on Atlantic City that he had already produced at a dozen other tracks. He helped attract the largest crowd the track had enjoyed since its first night of racing over a year earlier; the fans bet all his mounts with enthusiasm. In his first three tries, he managed one victory and two thirds. Then he entered the walking ring to greet Kelly and prepare for his ride in the stake on a speedy horse called Cinteelo. "I think you can control the pace," Kelly began. "There's only one other speed horse in here."

"No, the other speed horse was scratched," said Steve. "We should have the lead to ourselves."

"That," Kelly said as Steve led Cinteelo onto the track, "is what I call playing the game for keeps."

195

The race was uneventful, Cauthen seized the lead a few strides after the start and maintained his position all the way to the finish. "One trait that Steve shares with Shoemaker," Kelly said during the running, "is that when you see him in front, you just know he's got a ton of horse under him. He's always saving something for you." The comparison echoed one given by another thinking man's trainer, John Nerud: "Of all the jockeys I've seen in twenty-five years, the only two that consistently exhibit real intelligence are Shoemaker and Steve Cauthen."

But beyond such thoughtful assessments, the night in Atlantic City was an emotional one for Kelly. He had trained his very first horses at that track, and his appearance with Cinteelo was treated by old friends as a homecoming. Kelly's victory was sweet, and he enjoyed it even more when he watched an elderly man reach over the fence near the winner's circle and embrace and kiss his jockey. Cauthen appeared momentarily embarrassed, then managed a grin. But Kelly loved every minute of the scene.

"Did you see that?" Kelly kept asking. "When has racing had a hero that people wanted to kiss? I looked around at the fans who were cheering for Steve, and I saw bricklayers and executives, blacks and whites, men and young girls—all of them sensing that they are watching a real superstar. It's beautiful."

"Most of it's nice," said the kid. "But I can do without any more guys kissing me."

On the plane back to Saratoga, Cauthen slept soundly. His 12-hour day of work across two states was over. The next morning he would have to get up early to work the top two-year-old Affirmed for Laz Barrera. He deserved his rest, and sleep came quickly. But above the sound of the engines, trainer Kelly was still bubbling with infectious enthusiasm. "This little turkey keeps surprising you," he said. "He'll look up with that innocent smile of his and seem like such a little kid. And then he'll open his mouth and tell you something about a horse that will amaze you." The pressure of training thoroughbreds did not seem at all unbearable that late night for Tommy J. Kelly. And the kid sleeping in the seat behind him had a lot to do with it.

"You look at the number of horses that pass through Frank Martin's outfit," says Cauthen, "and you figure that he must take a lot out of his stock. But when you're close to the situation, you also see how often he wins with cripples. You see horses that can't even walk around the shed row one day, and then they win for Frank Martin the next day. He can fool you."

Rough, unkempt, and given to snarled guttural Spanish oaths, Pancho Martin is a contrast to some of the more cerebral-sounding horsemen in New York—and an unlikely-looking partner to be winning races with the baby-faced kid. But young Cauthen is only one of a long line of people who have been "fooled" or outwitted by Martin's feats with sore-legged animals. The Cuban-born trainer has been patching up cripples and winning with them since long before the kid was born.

A year before Steve's birth, to be precise, Martin saddled a long shot named Manassa Mauler in Aqueduct's big race of the spring, the Wood Memorial. The crowd was shocked when Manassa Mauler held off the favored First Landing to win. Then the astonishment spread at the scene in the winner's circle: long after his colt was led away, Martin stood nearby, shouting and handing out $20 bills to stable hands and friends.

Martin made his share of big scores in the years that followed, and if his impulsive generosity and love of celebrations didn't always manifest itself in the winner's circle, it was always evident around the racetrack's bars. Pancho could often be found paying tribute to a recent winner with one hand curled around a drink and the other pounding his own chest. "This horse has it here," he would growl. "In the heart. His legs ain't worth two dollars. But his heart, that belongs in stakes races."

When the horses had the heart, Martin had the touch to make the legs cooperate—at least enough to win some claiming races. In the 1960s, when his owners had limited budgets, he specialized in buying well-bred horses that had been discarded by more fashionable stables because of their infirmities. Greentree Stable sold one such horse, Rudolph, because he had knees "like melons," in Martin's words. But the knees responded to patient treatment in Pancho's barn, and Rudolph began winning. At about the same time, Alfred Gwynne Vanderbilt reluctantly gave up on a big, once-promising colt called Table Hopper.

Table Hopper was by Vanderbilt's champion Native Dancer out of the mare Buffet Supper. His blood was as rich as his name was clever, and as a two-year-old he had flashed stakes ability. Then his ankles betrayed him. After more than two years of caring for the colt, the Vanderbilt stable dropped him into a claiming race. Martin took him for $5000. There was no instant cure for Table Hopper's troubles, and Martin ran him seven times before he finally won—for a mere $3500. But that was just the beginning of one of the most remarkable training feats in the history of cheap horses.

Realizing that Table Hopper was feeling better than he had in years, Martin moved quickly to take advantage. He ran the horse three times within nine days, six times within a month; between races, Table Hopper was asked to do little but rest and walk around the barn. "You push them hard," Martin said, "then you give them a rest. It sounds easy. But you have to know when to push and when to stop." Pancho winked, making it clear that he knew those answers. Table Hopper won a piece of the purse in all but one of those races. Then he rested, returned—and scored three more victories. Martin had not only solidified the old knots and protuberances of Table Hopper's legs, but he had learned something else. The horse loved distance, and he didn't mind carrying weight.

Martin lost the horse when Buddy Jacobson claimed him for $6500. Jacobson began entering Table Hopper in "starter handicaps" for horses that have run for a $3500 claiming price. As the racing secretary began putting more weight on him to bring him back to his rivals, Table Hopper kept winning. But six weeks later Jacobson dropped him back into a regular claiming race. The price had now risen to $10,500. Martin took him anyway.

"He goes back in the handicaps now," said Pancho. "The weight shouldn't stop him. He's got too much class for those horses in thirty-five-hundred dollar starter handicaps." Pancho was right again. Table Hopper won one race under a staggering 129 pounds, and repeated under 132. When he was assigned 136 for his next try, Martin stormed into racing secretary Tommy Trotter's office and demanded, "What do you think he is? A steeplechase horse?" But he ran Table Hopper anyway, and the game gray managed to grab third money despite his burden. When Trotter dropped his weight assignment back to 133 for his next handicap, Table Hopper scored perhaps his greatest victory.

It took 138 pounds to finally stop him. An hour after Gun Bow had edged champion Kelso in one of the greatest Woodward Stakes ever run, Table Hopper walked onto the Aqueduct track carrying 12 pounds more than either Gun Bow or Kelso. In fact, handicap champions like Kelso and Tom Fool had built enduring reputations without ever carrying more than 136 pounds. The 138 pounds on Table Hopper was believed to be a record for the cheaper handicap ranks.

Jockey Bobby Ussery felt something go wrong in midstretch. Table Hopper was still digging in, trying to hurl his huge frame forward toward the leaders. But his action was not smooth and his head was bobbing slightly. Ussery did not punish him any more than necessary, and he was beaten by 13 lengths. When he returned to Martin's barn, there was a tenderness in the way he put his feet down on the ground, and his large gray head bobbed ominously. Pancho feared the worst, and in the next few days the fears were realized. For most of a year the trainer had been borrowing time, using all his wiles and medications to postpone the ending that was made inevitable by the infirmities in Table Hopper's legs. But Martin was also shrewd enough to sense that the fling was over. Few horses at any level at the major tracks ever win more than half a dozen races in a year. Table Hopper had won ten in that season. But he was not to win again.

"He still has the class," growled Pancho. "But the legs won't carry him any more. It's time to drop him down." Eventually he entered Table Hopper for a meager $4500 claiming price, and another man bought him. At the end of that year, on a bleak

December day at Aqueduct, Table Hopper made his last courageous run through the stretch. With an eighth of a mile to go, the chronically sore foot and the puffy ankle finally refused to carry any weight any farther. Oswaldo Rosado, riding him, felt the trouble and tried to pull up his mount. But Table Hopper had spent most of his seven years trying to run just a little harder than his legs should have allowed, and this time he tried so hard that before he could be stopped the bones of his right front leg were shattered. The race, the 46th of his career, was his last. A half hour later, in the dusk on the quiet backstretch, track veterinarian Manny Gilman thrust a large hypodermic needle into Table Hopper's neck, in the swiftest and most humane way anyone has devised for killing a hopelessly crippled racehorse.

For Pancho Martin that ending was only a distant echo. He had to be reminded of Table Hopper. "Oh yeah, I remember him," he finally said. "He was very good to me. But you can't sit around remembering the ones that are gone. You got to get rid of the ones whose time is up, and look for new ones to replace them—new ones with the same kind of class."

In recent years Martin's restless quest has become much easier. He now trains for millionaire real estate entrepreneur Sigmund Sommer. Martin and Sommer are a perfect team. Both like to drink and bet and brag about their successes. Most important, both love action. They have no interest in breeding a horse and waiting perhaps four years to learn what they have achieved; they are not even particularly good customers at yearling sales. They prefer to find a horse that is fully developed and ready to win; then they buy him and win with him. This strategy of speedy gratification might appeal to many people in a business that eventually strains everyone's patience. But no one has ever made it work quite the way Sommer and Martin do, because no one has ever spent money quite as fast as Sommer or churned out results as quickly as Martin.

At the high stakes that Sig Sommer brings to the game, racing is not always a pretty profession. Just as he once nursed the fragile legs of cheap claimers, Martin now takes great pride in getting the most out of better animals like Autobiography, which won a series of major stakes before a fatal accident at Santa Anita, and Turn and Count, which came all the way back from a bowed tendon to become a New York star under Cauthen. But Martin has also advised Sommer to purchase some six-figure horses that ran very slowly. And on at least one memorable occasion, fueled by cocktails and the encouragement of his troupe of hangers-on, Sommer ventured into the Saratoga yearling sale without Pancho—and walked away with a $250,000 colt that couldn't run at all.

Martin almost quit Sommer over that colt, the ironically named Tom Swift. There have been other flare-ups through the years. But for the most part the relationship is a good one, because Sommer provides the money and Martin adds the action. The way this team plays, the game may get expensive and infuriating. But it is never boring.

Martin loves claiming wars. When another horseman annoys him by claiming one of his horses or, worse yet, improving his performance, Pancho does not hesitate to begin claiming everything the other man enters. He knows that the rival will then start claiming his horses. But he is more than willing to match wits and bankrolls with anyone.

When the enemy is a small trainer, a Martin war can be cruel. Armed with Sommer's fortune, Martin can literally buy a man out of business before the rival can retaliate. But when he picks on someone his own size, Martin can precipitate some intriguing battles. For several years he has carried on a noisy feud with the equally volatile Johnny Campo, and there have been months when each man claimed every single horse that the other entered. There has been no clearcut winner in this running war: each man can point to horses that he has improved and to others that he foisted on the rival "idiot" or "nitwit" just as they were about to break down. But whatever its results, the war keeps tempers boiling and tension high—just the way horsemen like Martin and Campo like it best.

Such conditions only increase the natural pressures of the training profession—and make the jockey's position all the most precarious. Martin and Campo spend a good part of every working morning at Belmont in arguments with agents of jockeys who have allegedly ruined horses that should have been easy winners. Before the 1977 Kentucky Derby, Campo provided one of the most quoted comments ever made about a jock when he said of Seattle Slew's rider Jean Cruguet, "The Derby lasts for two minutes, and that's a long time for the Frenchman to go without screwing something up." For his part, Martin tends to greet agents with a sort of scattershot diatribe: "Your rider, does he ever win a photo? . . . I see that your rider is scared to go through holes these days . . . And yours, he could screw up a high mass . . ." But under racing's strange code of conduct, it is interesting to note that Campo still uses Cruguet and Martin ends up employing most of the riders that he so gleefully ridicules on the backstretch.

Martin's relationship with Cauthen began unsteadily. Shortly after the kid arrived in New York, he rode a horse for Pancho and encountered several traffic jams in the race. He finished far back, and the next morning Martin awaited Goodman with a stream of imprecations. "You think I'm running a school here?" Pancho barked. "You think you gonna bring some kid to learn how to ride while he gets my horses beat? Get out of here. I don't want to hear about this kid."

"You will, Frank," Goodman said softly. "You'll hear a lot. And you'll come around begging me to let him ride for you." Neither Martin nor Goodman ever does any begging, but Lenny did prove vaguely prophetic. Within months, Martin was winning races at a furious pace—and Steve was riding many of his winners. By the time Cauthen rode Turn and Count to win the $75,000 Grey Lag Handicap in March, the kid's baby face seemed almost as much a part of the Sommer-Martin image as the familiar green and gold silks.

At the time of Turn and Count's big win, Martin had amassed the remarkable total of 44 victories in 47 racing days. But only racing insiders noticed, because the general public was preoccupied with the kid's 124 winners during the same stretch. Similarly, two years earlier, Pancho had won 15 races in the opening week of the season, only to be upstaged by Angel Cordero, who won 22 during the same week to set the record that Cauthen would eventually break. Since most horsemen agree that training 15 winners is a lot more difficult than riding 22, Martin was once asked if he was bothered when his own feats were ignored in favor of performances by jockeys. "Bothered?" he said, keeping things in perspective. "God damn right I'm bothered."

In the feverish competition among top trainers, almost everyone is looking for the edge. Sometimes they search for it in a vial: every year, veterinary supply salesmen entice horsemen with some new analgesic or supplement that will "help" horses without vilating drug restrictions—or at least without being traceable by existing methods. Some trainers swear by the few vets who specialize in such things; others simply swear, when they are suspended after a lab test reveals the presence of some forbidden substance that was supposed to be untraceable.

Other trainers seek the edge in the elaborate bluffing of the claiming game: if you drop one horse way down in value and he breaks down, rivals may assume that your other "drop-downs" are also unsound. They will hesitate to claim from you, and you will win races without losing your horses.

Then there are more specific gimmicks. Laz Barrera, the gentleman trainer presumed to be above the street wars of the Martins and Campos, has been known to drop a horse far down in value and then bring him to the paddock in bandages halfway up to his neck. Many horses wear standing bandages before a race, to protect the legs or prolong the effect of the pain-dulling ice in which they have been standing back at the barn. But Barrera's bandages were not for standing; wrapped tight and secured with tape and pins, they were clearly for use in the race. Noticing this, other trainers assumed that the horse must be very infirm and in need of support. They decided not to claim him.

The deadline for submitting claims is 15 minutes before post time. When that time passed, most of the horses were leaving their paddock stalls to enter the walking ring. "Wait a minute," Barrera said to his groom. "Cut the bandages off him." Then Laz turned to a friend and winked. Minutes later the horse won the race easily—and returned unclaimed to the Barrera barn. "It's an old trick," the trainer chuckled. "But it can still be a good one, once in a while."

For betting stables, another edge comes from hiding workouts. This can be done by switching exercise riders or saddlecloths, simply lying to the clockers, or in its most picturesque form, by "daylighting," or working a horse before there is enough dawn light to make him visible. But the daylighting ploy has its perils. Some years ago a well-known Chicago trainer found himself with an unraced filly so fast that she could win a big bet for him at first asking. But the man wanted to be sure. And he wanted to get a good price. So he hid the filly from the clockers all summer in Chicago, and then he decided to hold her back a few weeks longer and make his score in Kentucky. One dark morning at Churchill Downs, he sent her out for a final predawn workout.

As the exercise boy guided the filly onto the track, the trainer drove his car through the underpass beneath the backstretch and onto the infield. Positioning himself near the half-mile pole, he waited for the sound of the filly's feet. When he heard her thunder past the pole, he clicked his watch, then turned his car and accelerated across the pitch-black infield toward the finish line. Unfortunately, he was still short of the finish line when he crashed head-on into a pole, wrecking his car.

Undaunted, the man climbed out of the rubble and scrambled to the finish line just in time to clock the workout: a fast half mile in 46 seconds. His car was a total loss, but at least his betting coup seemed imminent. Two days later the filly was entered. There was only one slow workout under her name in the *Racing Form*. The crafty trainer figured that her daylighting exploits would remain his little secret—until he had cashed his bet at handsome odds.

The filly won by five lengths. And paid $2.80 for a $2.00 bet. So much for dark little predawn secrets.

Some horsemen suspect that Pancho Martin and his son Jose have a different and more reliable edge in the claiming game. They suggest that the Martins benefit from a "Cuban mafia" of stable hands who filter them information about the critical ailments of horses that they might want to claim. This has never been proved. But if a Spanish stable hand were to benefit from Martin's impulsive generosity in the bars near Aqueduct, and then somehow seek to repay the favor, it would not come as a shock to many rivals. "People say those things because they're jealous," Martin says. "Mr. Hirsch Jacobs, when he started going good they accused him of using pigeon milk, right? Everyone who does good, somebody accuses of something, right?" Like Lenny Goodman on occasion, Pancho does not await answers to many of his questions. "You pick out a good horse, you sell a bad one to somebody," he continues. "That isn't cheating. That's being smart. That's what I call an edge."

For many trainers, Steve Cauthen became part of that edge. With a Kelly or a Martin, an Eclipse Award winner like Barrera or a little guy hoping desperately to win with the only horse in his barn, the kid maintained his pleasant attentive attitude. He listened to instructions, and much of the time he made them come true. There was no cause for yelling.

"Even when things don't go just right," says the kid, "all the trainers know that I'm always

207

trying. As long as I'm doing my best, it doesn't leave too much for them to complain about. And I guess I haven't made too many mistakes for them."

Eighteen

People are saying that time will take care
*   of people like me,*
That I'm livin' too fast and they say I can't
*   last for much longer.*
But little they see that their thoughts of
*   me are my savior,*
And little they know that the beat ought
*   to go a little faster.*
*   —*Willie Nelson, *Pick Up the Tempo*

The kid is neither a fast liver nor a rebel in
the Willie Nelson mold. But he knows the music,
and he is surely "country," and he understands the
special clock by which some people must live. He
knows that he is not doing what most people expect from a kid of his age. But he also knows, as
the great songwriter Nelson affirms in a different
context, that he must move on according to his
own rhythm. This is a sense that has something
to do with the South, and with setting goals that
seem foreign or impossible to the next kid in school

or the boyhood friends down the block. When you have decided to be the best race rider in the world, you cannot move to a designated tempo, or pause at the prescribed moments to savor the experience or take a rest. You must get on with it.

Steve Cauthen didn't need to read the books of Faulkner or sing the songs of Nelson to feel their spirit. It came to him from his father by way of Sweetwater, Texas, and New Orleans and all the other stops along the racetrack route. It was reinforced by a mother who understood what her son was doing and promised that win or loose, it would work out fine as long as he didn't let it change him. And so once he was past the twin crises of injury and the loss of his apprenticeship, once he was an accepted figure among the diverse trainers and the friendly rivals in the jockeys' room, the kid never thought about slowing down. The wheel was spinning and the sensation was good, and when he was asked about where it was taking him, the answer came quickly and easily: "I'm still doing just what I want to do."

The wheel moved in ever-widening circles, and before the great year was completed, the kid had ridden at 23 different tracks—and left his mark almost everywhere. Hilaleah was among the first to beckon. After some frantic bidding against neighboring Gulfstream, track management paid Goodman enough appearance money to get the kid—and the reward was a good opening-day crowd at the struggling track. Steve won only one race that day, but he left Floridians with a vivid memory of his ability: just after he rushed a horse called Vent du Nord to victory by a nose, the horse stumbled badly. Steve gathered him up without losing any of his extraordinary balance, and returned to the winner's circle with the familiar poker-faced expression. Local horsemen, inclined to be skeptical, shook their heads and muttered, "This is a pro."

At Penn National, near Harrisburg, Pennsylvania, there were tornado warnings when Steve arrived; he still attracted one of the largest crowds in the history of that innovative little track. Latonia, near his hometown, threw him a party and he celebrated by winning a race with a maiden that had lost 14 in a row. He helped Oaklawn Park in Arkansas to have its biggest day ever, and he stimulated business at other tracks from New England to California. Horses like Secretariat and Seattle Slew have proved to be major drawing cards on one-shot visits to racetracks. But a teenager on horseback turned out to be an even greater attraction.

"Every time I go to a new track for a day," the kid says, *"Lenny tells me, 'Don't worry, you're on six cinches.' Now, I know it can never work out that way. But riding in new places is fun, and I usually get my share of winners. The only real problem is meeting the press in each area. I mean, sometimes the reporters ask so many questions, you'd think I just got out of jail for killing somebody."*

If Steve sometimes had to resist an urge to "yell that I'd had enough," the reporters seldom noticed. Everywhere he went, they were impressed with his poise under fire. Once, for example, he agreed to tape a television commercial for Hialeah. He was supposed to say, "Welcome to the most beautiful track in the world." Instead, without cutting into his enthusiasm, he called it "one of the most beautiful." Somebody tried to reshoot it and correct it. Steve did it again, his own way. On or off the racetrack, he never let anyone push him into a position he wasn't ready to take.

At Saratoga in August, Steve passed another milestone. In the historic Whitney Stakes, a race that was supposed to showcase the mighty Forego, he steered Nearly on Time to a comfortable front-running victory. Forego, unable to handle the wet track, finished last. But the victory was especially sweet for Cauthen because the trainer of Nearly on Time was LeRoy Jolley, one of the hardboots who had always been particularly skeptical about the kid's talent. It also marked his 300th victory on the New York circuit, breaking Velasquez's old record of 299—with almost five full months remaining in the season.

Saratoga also produced some changes in Steve's stature. The chartist named Doc, who never did get over the experience of Steve's first ride on Monsi, sat under the elms one day and talked about it. "The kid doesn't dominate the way he used to," Doc said. "He's gone from changing the whole game around to being merely a great rider."

That was all right with Cauthen. Nobody could have continued to skew the betting and the results as he had when he was still an apprentice. He was content to be battling Cordero for the lead in the jockey standings, proving that he required no special edge to stay at the top. And gradually, he and Goodman were switching their emphasis from quantity to quality. Lenny was willing to pass up potential winning mounts in order to ride horses who seemed to have a future in big-money stakes. And Steve was proving that he could fit stakes horses just as smoothly as he could fit a recalcitrant maiden in a claiming race. Before the year ended, he had won 23 stakes races. And ridden two champions, Johnny D. and Affirmed.

At least once, the quest for quality produced a welcome dilemma. In the fall, Cauthen had to choose between two top two-year-olds, Affirmed and the Arlington Futurity winner Sauce Boat. "I was hoping to keep them apart for as long as possible, because they were both real nice colts," he he said. "But when they both entered the Champagne, I had to make a choice. I took Affirmed." Affirmed finished second to his archrival Alydar in the Champagne Stakes at Belmont, while Sauce Boat, sadly, suffered a chipped knee and broke down. But Steve's account of the situation reveals another phase of growing up. Once he had insisted that he would ride whatever Goodman selected. Now he was speaking in the first person. He still respected Goodman's judgment and valued him as an agent. But he had also seized control of his own destiny.

And in the case of Affirmed, what a destiny it was.

"It's a thrill to send a horse to the lead and rate him perfectly so he keeps going to the wire," says Cauthen. *"It's also exciting to save a horse and make one big run through the stretch. But I think the most satisfying feeling I can get on a horse is to hook up in a head-to-head duel with another good horse. I love the sense that two horses are really trying, giving it everything they have. Especially when my horse has just a little more to give."*

Affirmed and Alydar provided just that kind of horse races. And Affirmed always had plenty to give the kid.

The Affirmed story has all the elements of great racing drama. The colt was bred by Louis Elwood Wolfson. Almost two decades earlier, fi-

nancier Wolfson had entered racing as an owner
and made an immediate mark. By 1965, he even
owned a Horse of the Year, the gritty little gelding
Roman Brother. But Wolfson had even more impact off the track. An aggressive and imaginative
businessman in a sport that sometimes seems so-
cially stagnant, Wolfson took an initiative in
lobbying for better tax breaks for racing, trying to
improve conditions for stable help, and generally
leading the sport forward.

Then Lou Wolfson was convicted of selling
unregistered stock and sentenced to a year in prison. When he emerged he kept a lower profile,
and racing was deprived of some valued leader-
ship. Now in his 60s, graying and dignified, Wolfson is married to the former Patrice Jacobs, the
charming daughter of the immortal horseman
Hirsch Jacobs. Patrice has spent her life amid the
trophies and the excitement of her family's achievements in racing, so the match seems ideal. Joe
Palmer once remarked wryly that the term "horse
lover" was truly applicable only to a horse in love
with another horse. But Lou and Patrice Wolfson
seemed to give the definition a new twist. They
were people in love with horses as well as each
other.

Still, it stretched the imagination to suspect
that the Wolfsons could come up with a champion
—particularly in the case of Affirmed. His sire,
Exclusive Native, was a son of Wolfson's great
racehorse Raise a Native, but only a modest success in his own right. Won't Tell You, the dam of
Affirmed, dropped six foals prior to that colt without producing a stakes horse. (In one more fascinating example of the strangely crossing patterns
of the track, one of her offspring was the claimer
Little Miracle, Cauthen's mount on his return from
his injury.) In contrast to Affirmed, his rival Aly-

dar was by the mighty Raise a Native himself, out
of Sweet Tooth, the dam of the 1977 champion
filly Our Mims.

But early in the game, Affirmed tended to
sprint away from other weanlings and yearlings on
Wolfson's Ocala, Florida, farm. When he began
training, first under Laz Barrera's brother Willie
and then in the care of Laz himself, he showed
that he was an outstanding prospect. He broke
his maiden, at long odds, under Bernie Gonzalez,
an apprentice who had been in Cauthen's shadow.
Then he won one stake in New York under Cordero, another in California under Laffit Pincay.
When he returned to New York, Cordero was
scheduled to ride him again. But fate—in the form
of Cordero's commitment to ride another promising
colt named Darby Creek Road—brought Affirmed
together with Cauthen.

Steve rode Affirmed for the first time in the
Sanford Stakes at Saratoga. "He tired to bear out
the whole trip," the kid said. Down the backstretch, Cauthen had to struggle to control his colt.
But when he finally got him straightened away in
the run to the wire, he was able to steer him down
the middle of the racetrack to victory. Ten days
later, after he had worked the colt once in the
morning, Steve found Affirmed much easier to handle. He seized the lead at the top of the stretch,
and when Alydar made his bid on the outside,
Affirmed accelerated and won by half a length.

It was a particularly memorable moment for
Patrice Jacobs Wolfson. Through all the glorious
years with her father, Patrice's favorite horse had
been Hail to Reason, the grand colt who had gone
on to sire many Jacobs stars. On his way to the
two-year-old championship, Hail to Reason had
also won the Hopeful—in 1960, the year when
Steve Cauthen was born. "Congratulating Stevie,"

said Patrice, "made me think of those seventeen years. I felt like a little old lady." But the fact was that she didn't look or really feel all that old. Entering the winner's circle, she was walking back into the most cherished experiences of her life. The kid was bringing it all together for her.

Gun Bow and Kelso, two magnificent handicap horses, once raced head-to-head for almost the entire distance of the mile-and-one-quarter Woodward Stakes. Jaipur and Ridan, two big three-year-olds, did the same thing in perhaps the greatest Travers Stakes ever run. Racing history is rich in tales of gut-wrenching duels between top horses of equal ability. But hardly anyone could recall a year in which a pair of two-year-olds was as well matched, and as brilliant, as Affirmed and Alydar. The Futurity at Belmont provided the next stage for their rivalry—and perhaps the best example of the talents of Affirmed and his rider.

The early pacesetter was a long shot, Rough Sea. But Cauthen stalked the leader along the rail, and Eddie Maple moved Alydar into close contention on the outside. Approaching the far turn of the seven-furlong race, Cauthen moved to the front along the rail. Alydar moved with him on the outside, and the battle was joined. In mid-stretch, jockey Eddie Maple got Alydar to the lead—and horses who take the lead on the outside at Belmont are seldom beaten by rivals along the rail. To make matters worse, the contenders were close together, and Cauthen had little room to flail his whip.

But the kid is not a flailer. With his crisp economy of motion, he managed to sting Affirmed repeatedly in the stretch drive. Inch by inch, Affirmed gained ground. Nearing the wire, he moved out by a nose, then a head. At the finish, Maple got one final lunge out of Alydar. But it fell short. Cauthen and Affirmed prevailed by a nose. "It was a real thrill," says Steve. "I'll never forget that race."

Neither would Maple, who lost the mount on Alydar to Velasquez after the race. It was difficult to imagine how trainer John Veitch could fault the rider for losing a great race by a nose. But a month later in the Champagne, the change in riders seemed to pay dividends. Velasquez guided Alydar down the middle of a muddy racing strip to a clear victory over Affirmed. "My horse ran OK," says Steve, "but he didn't really like the track. Jorge had clear sailing on the outside and he just blew by us." After the Champagne, the tally in head-on confrontations stood at three victories for Affirmed, two for Alydar. But Alydar had won the richest and most prestigious race in the Champagne. The championship, it turned out, would hinge on their final meeting in the Laurel Futurity.

Like fight managers, the two shrewd trainers plotted strategy for the season's climax. "Affirmed is tough," said Alydar's man Veitch. "You don't want to dog him and try to wear him down. You want to sneak up on him and hit him over the head."

"Alydar won't sneak up on Affirmed again," retorted Barrera. "In the Champagne, Steve was in between horses when Alydar made his big run on the outside. By the time Affirmed saw him, it was too late. But Alydar didn't continue to gain on Affirmed after Affirmed saw him."

Cauthen had a similar thought. "I don't want anyone between us this time," he said. "I want my horse to see him at all times, because what he sees, he usually beats. And this time I've got the outside position and I plan to keep it. I want to make sure that Affirmed always has a good view of Alydar."

The plans worked out very well. And the result was what most observers considered the best horse race of the year. Steve made the first important move, grabbing the lead from the front-runner, Star de Naskra, on the far turn. Alydar responded quickly. But Cauthen kept his mount far off the rail, giving Velasquez no choice but to stay inside him. Soon both stars left Star de Naskra far behind them and turned the Laurel Futurity into the decisive match that had been anticipated.

"There are a lot of races that never develop the way you'd hoped," says Steve. "So it's beautiful when one of them turns out the way you expected—especially when it's a big one. The Laurel race was that kind. I didn't want anybody between us and Alydar, distracting Affirmed. I also wanted to be outside. And I got both wishes. After that, I figured Affirmed would get the job done."

At the eighth pole the leaders were heads apart, in the midst of a repeat of their earlier duels. Cauthen and Velasquez both rode flawlessly; Affirmed and Alydar responded to the strokes of the whips with almost synchronized grace. "But during the last eighth," says Steve, "I always thought I had him. It was the first time in all our races that I was on the outside, and I think both those colts prefer to be out there. So I had the edge, and I felt good." Each time the two colts hit the ground with their front legs, the gap between them varied. Affirmed by a neck, then only by a head. But at the wire, the kid thrust Affirmed's head down as he had in 400–odd other finishes with other winners, and the final margin was a neck. Affirmed was the winner, and the champion.

And still the beat kept getting faster. If the

two Futurities were the most exciting races of the kid's life, the subsequent Washington D.C. International victory of Johnny D. brought him even wider acclaim. Then he got aboard Johnny D. again in Aquaduct's Turf Classic, and clinched the grass-racing championship for the colt with another brilliant ride. At about the same time, he encountered a slump in New York; for several weeks, he settled for only a winner or two each afternoon. Once he lost 22 races in a row. The rumors spread quickly as the vultures circled: the kid had gone too far too fast; he had discovered girls and the nightlife; he was getting complacent. Then, on a late November afternoon at Aqueduct, he silenced the doubters. For the third time, he accomplished what no one else had ever done more than once. He won six races in a day.

"It's hard to concentrate on writing," I told the kid one afternoon, "when I can keep winning money just by betting on horses like Johnny D."

"Write the book," said Steve, "so we can make some money that we can be sure about."

With the blend of reluctance, whimsy, and experimentation to which every adolescent is entitled, the kid was growing up. But he had to do it in full view of all of us. His wardrobe reflected his ambiguities. It is unlikely that he would have bought his Conair to blow-dry his hair back in Walton, or acquired the various cosmetics that jockeys apply as they depart the room each day. But even as he used the grown-up appliances and lotions that he picked up from other riders, the kid clung to his blue jeans and his soft country cap. While others, out of habit, insisted on lugging their heavy equipment bags from track to track, Steve hitched his own to one of those rolling carts that stewardesses use to get quickly through airports. "He's the superstar," joked one fellow rider, "and he looks like one of those guys walking an imaginary dog when he pushes that little cart around."

Some time around the Saratoga meeting, Steve also noticed that girls were interested in more than his autograph. He began to find time for occasional dates, and by the time he reached California for his second winter meeting, he found several girls that he enjoyed spending time with. The critics again seized on every situation, waiting for him to fall into the traps that had claimed so many other young riders. "But I'm just going out to dinner or a movie like any other kid my age would do with a girl," he said. "I wish I could do it without anybody making a big deal of it."

"If he wasn't interested in girls at this point," said Tex Cauthen, "I guess that would be a reason for me to worry."

In the jockeys' room Steve got a rough-cut education about women—about the same kind of education that he might have gotten if he had become an apprentice mechanic or truck driver as a teenager. A few swaggering riders boasted of their prowess. Others joked about women, and still others talked seriously about the problems of keeping families together while a person is irritable from dieting, traveling, or losing photo finishes. The most remarkable counsel probably came from the jockeys'-room jester, Jacinto Vasquez.

"Don't be like too many jocks, Steve," Jacinto said. "Too many young guys, they make some money and they find the first girl that really makes them happy, and they figure, 'Is this what it's all about?' And they marry her. And if they do it too quick, they regret it forever."

The kid was only half listening. He was busy

rummaging in a compartment of his locker, seeking a candy bar.

"I'll tell you one thing, Steve," Jacinto concluded. "A bad woman can be like the neutron bomb. Leaves all the buildings standing, ruins all the men."

The kid made a funny face and then broke into a high-pitched giggle. Then he pulled the wrapper off the O Henry bar that he had discovered deep in his locker, and began to chew on it.

The man-child is in a precarious position. The magazine *Children's Express,* which is staffed by children, sends two 12-year-olds and a 10-year-old to interview him, and they come away with the conclusion, "He's an ordinary kid, just like us." The celebrity magazines also call, and sometimes the smooth, mature answers he gives them make him sound different from the kid that he knows he is. Even for a kid whose main worry is his next high-school exam, being a teenager isn't easy. For Steve Cauthen, it can be difficult to sort out being a man and being a boy, living in private or living in the glare of constant attention.

But as he steps up to receive the awards, as he ventures into new territory and even settles for second place instead of first in the jockeys' standings on occasion, the kid seems equipped to handle it all. Tex and Myra Cauthen taught their eldest son very early that the world would not always hold six winners in an afternoon. He knows that he will make mistakes, hear boos, feel exhausted by the demands of the press and the public. But he also knows that there will always be a chance to recoup. As long as he doesn't grow too big or suffer some serious injury, there will always be another horse to ride. And when that part of his life ends, there will be more. Perhaps he will train horses, or breed them with some of the money that he is saving. Back in the farmhouse in Walton, his decision won't matter. The important thing is that he will return the way he left. Myra Cauthen, flashing that warm quizzical smile, will like that.

"When I read the stuff about me getting spoiled, I just turn the page," says Steve. "It doesn't bother me. But what really bugs me is when people start writing about me like I was a god. I don't have any magic. I have to prove myself like everybody else, as a race rider and as a person."

Some race rider. Some person. Some kid.

Epilogue: The Derby

In the early morning quiet of the Churchill Downs stable area, someone asked trainer Laz Barrera perhaps the silliest question of Kentucky Derby Week, 1978: "Are you worried about entrusting your Derby horse to an eighteen-year-old who's never ridden in this race before?"

"Worried? You kidding?" Barrera snorted and twisted his darkly handsome face into a grimace. But then he smiled and answered patiently. "Maybe some people still don't understand. Steve Cauthen is no eighteen-year-old. He's an old man. Sometimes he makes me believe in reincarnation. Maybe he had another life, where he was a leading rider for fifty years. That's how much he knows about his business."

There were chuckles in the group around Barrera, and the trainer warmed to his audience and went on in a happy jumble of Spanish, English, and mixed metaphors. "Maybe Steve is the thousand-year-old man," he concluded. "Maybe he *came to us as a gift from some other planet—in a flying sausage."*

There has always been a touch of whimsy in the relationship of Barrera, Cauthen, and their Derby colt Affirmed. Laz recalls how it all began, when Lenny Goodman first brought Steve to the Barrera barn at Belmont late in 1976. That year, Laz had captured the Derby with Bold Forbes. "I saw them coming," says the trainer, "and I figured, 'Oh, some friend of Lenny's must have sent his little kid to see Bold Forbes." I said I'd be glad to meet this little kid."

"No," Goodman corrected Laz that morning. "This isn't just somebody's kid. This is my new rider."

"Hoo, Lenny, you gonna go to jail for this," said Barrera. "This kid looks like he's twelve."

By the time Cauthen had turned 17 and ridden Affirmed to seven victories in eight races leading up to the Derby, there had been many more laughs. But as the big race approached, the flights of fancy became less frequent. For anyone lucky enough to have a top three-year-old, springtime in Kentucky is a time to get serious.

Cauthen celebrated his 18th birthday five days before the 1978 Kentucky Derby, and most of his years had been spent getting reading for his first Derby ride. Barrera turned 53 the day after the race, and had already distinguished himself as a Derby master with Bold Forbes. But there was no generation gap between the Kentucky kid and the Cuban-born horseman. During the winter in California, Cauthen had shared an apartment with Laz's son Larry. Back in New York he was living with another Barrera son, Albert. He and Laz had long shared a sense of family. And as the prerace pressure built, they were brought even closer by their sense of mission.

The road to Kentucky was not a smooth one for anyone around Affirmed. After his championship victory over Alydar at Laurel the previous fall, Barrera had given Affirmed a refreshing vacation and allowed him to unwind almost completely. He had planned to begin his cautious, painstaking preparation for the Derby in January 1978 at Santa Anita. With time and a fast horse on his side, Laz wanted to use both to perfection.

Then the elements wrecked the plan and robbed Barrera of his time. The winter was the rainiest in California history, and there were entire weeks when the waterlogged track was unsafe for galloping and Affirmed had to be content with walks and jogs inside the barn. Even when the Santa Anita maintenance crew managed to get the training track into decent shape for workouts, Barrera hesitated to use it. To travel from the barn to the training track, Affirmed would have to go through a tunnel. Barrera had a nightmarish premonition that his prized colt might rear up and smash his head in that tunnel. So most mornings, he kept Affirmed in the barn.

If this seems like negative thinking, it is only because that is the kind of thinking that good horses force upon good horsemen. Alydar's articulate young trainer John Veitch expressed this factor very well before the Derby: "Worrying goes with the job," he said. "The better things go with your horse, the more you fear that on the way from Keeneland to Churchill Downs, your van driver will have to jam on his brakes on the Interstate and your horse will be thrown off balance in the truck. There are so many little things that can go wrong—and you just have to try to anticipate every one of them and avoid them."

Barrera did avoid any freakish accidents. But the delays caused still other perils. "I've never had to train a horse this way in my life," he said. "Instead of taking sixty days to get him ready for his first race, I had to do it in forty-five. Before his first race in California, I had to work him faster than I wanted. That's a very easy way to overtrain a horse. So once I got him ready to run, I had to back off with him again."

This strategy produced some puzzling results. Affirmed won his first race, a sprint, with ease. But in his next effort, at a mile and a sixteenth, he had to struggle to beat lightly regarded rivals. Two weeks later, with Laffit Pincay, Jr., substituting for Cauthen because Steve was under suspension for careless riding, Affirmed won the important Santa Anita Derby in more impressive fashion. But the Hollywood Derby, the colt's last race before he reached Kentucky, brought more problems and controversy.

First there was the question of why Affirmed ran at Hollywood Park at all. Through the years, California-based horses have often fared poorly in Kentucky. The California colts who have won at Churchill Downs—including Barrera's Bold Forbes —have usually traveled east for their final Derby prep races. No horse in history had ever come directly from a Hollywood Derby victory to the winner's circle at Churchill Downs. The record showed that the time-honored routes to the Kentucky Derby were the Bluegrass Stakes at Keeneland in Lexington and the Wood Memorial at Aqueduct in New York. But while favorite Alydar was winning the Bluegrass by 13½ lengths and contender Believe It was boosting his stock by taking the Wood, Barrera defied the accepted pattern and stayed in the West.

"I thought about the long plane ride to New York for the Wood," explained Barrera. "I thought about the chance I would take each time I had to ship this horse. And I thought about my chance to win a good race for $250,000 right where I was in California. I knew people would talk about my decision. But I knew what I was doing."

People did talk, often with raised eyebrows, when Affirmed was less than overwhelming at Hollywood. "The only way we can lose this race," Barrera told Cauthen that day, "is to get blocked or get into some kind of trouble. So I want you to send him to the front and keep him in the clear. Also, I think maybe we've been babying him too much. Today, let him get used to being whipped."

Cauthen followed the instructions with his usual precision. Setting a swift early pace, he raced the promising Radar Ahead into defeat, opened up a clear lead and then began whipping. In all, he hit his mount 12 times coming through the stretch. But beneath him, Affirmed seemed to wonder what the kid was getting so excited about. With no horses moving up to challenge him, the colt was content to lope through the final furlongs in moderate time. He won by only two lengths.

Each slash of Steve's whip that afternoon gave the critics new ammunition. Some speculated that the two-year-old horse had simply not developed much as a three-year-old. Others questioned his competitive fire. Woody Stephens, the respected trainer of Believe It, went so far as to say at Churchill Downs, "I don't know about Affirmed. He kind of looks like he's all legs this year."

The only people who weren't worried were the ones who counted. "Affirmed was just playing," said Cauthen. "He was flopping his ears back and forth in the stretch, and looking around for something to beat. I don't care what it looked like from the stands. From where I sit, it seems that Laz is bringing him up to every race a little stronger than he was before. I think I can do anything I want with him when I have to."

Barrera himself was puzzled and sometimes angered by his curious position. His colt had started 13 times in his life, with 11 victories and 2 second-place finishes behind Alydar. He had beaten Alydar four times. He had also earned more than $700,000—more money than any horse ever won before starting in a Kentucky Derby. But he was not even the favorite in Kentucky. "This is a crazy business," said Laz. "What does Affirmed have to do to make people believe in him? Everybody is saying what's wrong with this horse. Am I the only one who can see so much that's right with him?"

Training became a lonely art for Barrera with Affirmed. When he wasn't hearing public criticism about the colt's races, Laz also had to endure some private agonies. Early in the winter, Affirmed suffered some soreness in his rippling muscles. It was nothing serious, but it did demand attention and treatment while precious mornings slipped away. Then there was the heart-grabbing moment when the colt, feeling frisky and full of himself, bucked an exercise rider off his back and galloped loose on the Santa Anita track until he could be gathered in by an outrider. He was unharmed, but the incident underscored the message that this Derby campaign was not going to be a relaxing one for Barrera.

To make matters more confusing, while Affirmed was dodging raindrops and potential disasters, his archrival Alydar was positively blooming in the Florida sun. In contrast to the well-made but somewhat light-bodied Affirmed, Alydar was a strapping colt who thrived on hard work. "If he didn't work hard," said trainer Veitch, "he would eat up his feed and blow up like a balloon. This kind of hard-trying colt makes training a pleasure most of the time. Naturally, I still have to beware of the fine line between doing enough with him and doing too much. But so far, everything's been going according to schedule."

Alydar's first start at Hialeah was brilliant. His second, in the prestigious Flamingo Stakes, was absolutely devastating. Then, in the Florida Derby at Gulfstream, Alydar encountered a strong challenge from the good colt Believe It—and drew away in the stretch with the kind of lordly disdain that often marks champions. Since most handicappers rated Believe It as superior to anything that Affirmed was beating in California, the triumph seemed a significant one for Alydar. And for those who break down Derby dreams into the cold numbers of handicapping, Alydar showed the ability to burst an eighth of a mile in 11 seconds any time jockey Jorge Velasquez asked him for speed.

But like Affirmed with his kid rider, Alydar offered a rich racing drama along with the numbers. He was owned by the Calumet Farm of Admiral and Mrs. Gene Markey—the farm whose devil's-red and blue silks had been carried by eight Kentucky Derby winners. Lucille and Gene Markey were octogenarians confined to wheelchairs and unable to attend their colt's races in Florida. But infirmities and Mrs. Markey's failing eyesight had not curtailed their graciousness, high spirits, or enthusiasm for racing.

At the Bluegrass Stakes, the Calumet tradition hung palpably in the Kentucky air. The beautiful Calumet Farm, with its immaculate white fences and barns trimmed with devil's red, is the next-door neighbor of the historic Keeneland track in Lexington, Kentucky. Keeneland officials arranged for the Markeys to be driven to trackside in a station wagon so they could glimpse Alydar's final Derby prep. After that victory, Velasquez guided the colt over to his owners and greeted them warmly. At a track that takes its traditions seriously, there were more than a few moist eyes. The Markeys do not have any heir with any interest in racing, and Lexington real estate developers may already be looking greedily at Calumet's prized acreage. But for that one bright day at Keeneland, Alydar seemed to be the colt who could hold off any such unwelcome "progress." The glory era of Calumet, which had begun when the immortal trainer Plain Ben Jones won the 1941 Derby with Whirlaway, seemed alive and well in the care of Veitch and Velasquez. And many Kentuckians felt that the Markeys richly deserved this final Derby fling.

Certainly Kentucky was proud of its kid from Walton. But Cauthen would have many chances in the Derby. For Calumet, time was running out. It also happened that Affirmed was an outsider, bred in Florida and raced in California—while Alydar was a solid citizen of the bluegrass country. Reading the local papers and talking with those who so admired the Markeys, it was easy to see that in this Derby, Alydar would be the betting favorite. He was the "home team."

"*Racing in California all winter was a new experience for me,*" *Cauthen said that spring.* "*I was riding against the best bunch of jocks I've ever seen in one place. And I rode a lot of long shots. When I was hot in New York, I'd get on horses that should have been thirty to one and they'd be eight to one. In California, with guys like Shoemaker and Pincay and Darrel McHargue against*"

*me, my thirty-to-one shots would stay thirty to one.
And most of them would run about that way."*

In some ways, Cauthen's pre-Derby campaign
paralleled that of Affirmed. He performed well and
felt satisfied. But because he was somewhat less
dazzling than he had been earlier in his career,
outsiders kept wondering if something was wrong.

Steve's main problem in California was one of
simple logistics. Most West Coast horsemen campaign year round in that area, and they prefer to
employ riders who are also permanent residents.
A trainer with stakes horses likes to plan for the
long run. So when one is faced with a choice between several star jockeys, he tends to select a
Pincay or a McHargue, who will be available any
time, over a kid—even a Cauthen—who will be
back in New York within a few months.

Agent Goodman was aware of the situation
when he took Steve to the Coast, and in some
cases he overcame it: Steve won major stakes not
only with Affirmed but with J. O. Tobin from
Barrera's barn and Noble Dancer II for Tommy
Kelly. But he made relatively few inroads into the
year-round California stables, and so he inevitably
rode fewer winners than he had in New York. In
some circles this was interpreted as a slump. At
one point, as Steve fell far behind the red-hot
McHargue in the jockey standings, a *Daily Racing
Form* headline even proclaimed, CAUTHEN OFF TO
SLOW START. After four months of 1978, this slow
start had held him to winnings of $1.8 million—
leaving him a little below the $6 million pace he
had set a year earlier.

Then there was the unusual case of Steve's
suspension—his first since his apprentice days. The
incident occurred in a race in which he finished

231

out of the money, and unlike most suspensions, it was not precipitated by a foul claim by another rider. But the Santa Anita stewards noticed on the patrol films that Cauthen had "failed to keep a straight course" in the run down the backstretch—and slapped him with five days on the sideline.

A bizarre tangle of legal and administrative hearings ensued. In an effort to keep the mount on Affirmed in his second race of the year, Cauthen and Goodman hired a lawyer and won a stay of the suspension in court. But that ploy backfired when the case was reviewed and the suspension upheld: Steve had saved the mount in the relatively minor San Felipe Handicap, only to be forced to serve his penalty later and miss the important Santa Anita Derby. The hearings also produced some surprising twists. To Steve's dismay, the prime witness against him turned out to be Bill Shoemaker. Lenny Goodman left the scene grumbling, "I'm glad I'm a good agent. I don't think I'd like being a lawyer." And then Barrera tried to use the utmost diplomacy in replacing the kid—only to have that gesture backfire, too.

"I have two good riders and friends of mine who can ride instead of Steve," Barrera said. "We'll get together with Laffit Pincay and Angel Cordero, and flip a coin." The riders seemed to go along. But after Pincay won the toss, Cordero's agent Tony Matos decided that he had never liked the coin-flip idea. Matos exchanged stormy words with Barrera and stalked away. Affirmed's subsequent victory assuaged some of the bruised feelings in the horse's camp. But the affair represented an interesting phase in the ongoing process of growing up on the racetrack: a lesson in human nature—and in knowing who your friends are.

Knowing who his girlfriends were turned out

to be much easier. Along with Larry Barrera, Steve began to date more frequently in California. "I like these California girls," he said. "You treat them nice and take them to nice places, and you can have a good time for a few days. But then they leave you alone. They don't try to interfere with your life or your business." Clearly, Steve had listened well to the best advice from his elders on the subject. Women were not about to alter his style or damage his career. But that didn't stop a few rumors from arising—particularly in one New York paper that announced that he was in love and planning to stay year round in California. "That reporter seemed to think that as long as girls weren't changing me, he'd do it for me," Steve complained. After such strange winter happenings, there were moments when the high-tension atmosphere of Louisville in Derby Week seemed almost calm to the kid.

"Affirmed," Steve kept insisting to the doubters, "happens to be the smartest horse in the world."

The words were sincere, but as Steve repeated them, he unwittingly brought down added pressure on himself. The Kentucky Derby is not only the most exciting two minutes in sports. It is also the most meticulously analyzed two-minute period. For days before the event, serious handicappers and once-a-year racegoers debate about which horses will go to the lead, come from behind—or win. To many of those observers the 1978 Derby seemed to hinge largely on what the so-called smart horse would do.

For trainers and riders of the other three contenders, no such deep thinking seemed required. Alydar was a strong finisher and Believe It had spent the spring learning to come from behind in similar fashion; if they made closing bids that fell short, there would be no cause for second-guessing and claiming that they should have changed their successful styles. Sensitive Prince, at the other extreme, was a naturally aggressive speed horse. Master trainer Allen Jerkens had worked patiently to teach him to relax and conserve his energy. But nobody really expected him to be anywhere but in front in the early stages of the Derby.

Affirmed was the colt who defied such predictions. He had sprinted to the lead in some races and relaxed off the pace in others. It was generally agreed that he would accept whatever strategy Barrera and Cauthen dictated. But that choice of strategy struck some as the key to the outcome. If Cauthen challenged Sensitive Prince early and was later overhauled by Alydar, he could be accused of a serious error. If he laid back and tried to make his run alongside Alydar as he had done so well with Affirmed as a two-year-old, he might allow Sensitive Prince to steal the race. Along with Barrera, it was Steve's job to find just the right compromise and execute it with perfect timing. Any mistake would leave him open to criticism. Riding such a smart horse, it seemed, was an easy way to get oneself outsmarted.

"I'm not worried about anybody second-guessing me," said Steve. "I'm not even thinking about what will happen if we lose. I'm thinking about how I'll feel when we win."

Shortly after Affirmed's arrival at Churchill Downs, Barrera began applying the finishing touches. He sent the colt out for a casual mile-and-one-eighth workout.

"He don't need too much work now," he said. "I want him to go a slow mile and then open up a

234

little the last eighth." The mile was slow, but the last eighth took a crisp 12 seconds. Barrera walked back to his barn with a smile.

"He went pretty slow," somebody said. "Are you worried about him having enough speed?"

"I'm never worried about his speed."

A few days later Affirmed breezed five furlongs in much faster time. The next question was inevitable: "Are you afraid he went too fast?"

"I'm never worried about this horse," he said firmly. "About anything."

Lou and Patrice Wolfson watched the workouts with sparkling eyes. Before arriving in Kentucky, both had some misgivings about the Derby adventure. Wolfson knew that among the endless prerace questions, he would have to face some inquiries about the legal difficulties that he had hoped to put behind him forever by serving his time. Patrice feared that reporters who recalled her great father, Hirsch Jacobs, would place too much emphasis on her at the expense of her husband, who had bred and raised their horse. At times both problems arose. Wolfson's wheeler-dealer background, in particular, was compared unkindly to the aristocratic mien of the owners of Alydar. But Wolfson handled the tough questions with a dignity that changed some minds about him, Patrice was unfailingly charming—and soon both were happily anticipating the one victory that had always eluded both Wolfson's stable and the wonderful Mr. Jacobs.

Derby week tends to generate a rising dramatic tension all its own. As workouts are concluded and there is little to do but stand around the barns and wait, voices are amplified, nerves are jangled, and tempers can flare. That is what happened on the morning when Affirmed drew the number two post position and Alydar drew number ten. Both trainers had wanted to be on the outside, where their jockeys could stalk their rivals most easily.

"God gave me number two," said Barrera evenly. "So I guess I better be happy with it."

Over at his own barn, John Veitch was jubilant. "I like where my horse is," he said. "And I love where Affirmed is, down on the inside. Cauthen may have to use his colt earlier than he wants in order to get position. Or he may get trapped when the speed horses begin to stop in front of him."

Within minutes the comments were relayed to Barrera, who let his Latin blood boil all the way to the surface. "You go tell John Veitch to train his own horse and stop trying to train mine," he snapped. "That's babyish to guess what will happen in a race. The year Bold Forbes won, some nut threw a smoke bomb on the track. Did anyone guess that would happen? Once those gates open, nobody in America can tell what's gonna happen."

But moments later, in the fantastic atmosphere that surrounds all Derby debates, Laz found himself musing, like Veitch, on exactly what would happen when the gates opened. Suddenly a visitor who moved quickly enough between the stalls occupied by the two favorites could have imagined himself listening to the counterclaims of fighters at a championship weigh-in.

"Steve can place Affirmed wherever he wants," Barrera was saying.

"If Steve has to move too early, his horse might get rank under him and not want to ease back," Veitch was arguing.

"Steve will probably lay third behind Sensitive Prince and that cheap speed horse, Raymond Earl," said Barrera.

"Velasquez will be a few lengths behind Cauthen and outside him, where he can see what

Affirmed is doing and then try to burst past him when it's time," said Veitch. Someone mentioned the remarkable statistic that if all six of their earlier races had been strung together, Alydar and Affirmed would have raced four miles and two furlongs—and finished just a neck apart. Affirmed's neck.

"But this is a new year," said Veitch. "Right, Aly?"

Alydar snorted loudly. "That's the sound," said Veitch, laughing "of a horse that's run four good races and is ready for more."

"Affirmed will take the lead at about the head of the stretch," Barrera was saying at about the same moment. "Then Alydar will start to come at him, and it should be a hell of a Derby. May the best horse win—again."

The stable area began to empty and Laz Barrera prepared to ride to his hotel, and the clever quips and predictions faded quickly. It was a gray silent morning and Barrera's voice was low as he resumed talking. "There was an item in the Racing Form *this week," he said. "It was about three kids, jockeys in New York who could have been something. They're all suspended for taking drugs. Cocaine or something, I hear. But it was just a little item, under the stewards' rulings in the fine print."*

The Derby trainer paused. "You know, that should have been a big story, not a little note in the paper. As big as Stevie Cauthen trying to win the Derby. So every kid in the country could see how for every great kid like Steve, there are stupid kids who will throw their whole careers away for nothing. Little kids should think about that once in a while when they look at Steve. Racing is the greatest sport in the world, the greatest life in the world. It can give you everything you ever dreamed about.

*But you have to really work for it. And really love it.
The minute you start taking anything for granted,
thinking you're bigger than the game, it makes you
pay. People who follow all the stories about Stevie,
they should read about that other side too."*

Barrera knows all about the work and the love.
He came from Cuba by way of Mexico. He has
been in America for about two decades, working
mainly with cheap horses. But his thoroughness and
talent gradually caught many eyes, and over the
years, admiring owners like Emil Dolce and the
late Eddie Burke gave him stakes horses to train.
He got results, and finally, from Puerto Rico, he
got Bold Forbes. Laz's Derby victory with the
flashy Bold Forbes was memorable, but it was
overshadowed five weeks later: horsemen as brilliant as Allen Jerkens have suggested that Barrera's
feat of stretching the sprinter Bold Forbes out to
win the mile-and-one-half Belmont Stakes may have
been the single greatest training feat of our generation.

Now Barrera looms as a likely fixture at classic
races. His present owners have money to spend and
his horses have pedigrees—and these are two conditions that he has not always enjoyed in his profession. But Barrera was taking nothing for granted
at Churchill Downs with Affirmed. If anything, he
seemed more intense than he had been on his first
visit with Bold Forbes. He wanted this Derby badly, for the Wolfsons and the kid, and for the things
he believed in most strongly in racing. Forget about
Laz's crafty training tricks. We're talking about the
work and the love.

At last it was time: 5:41 p.m. on the first
Saturday in May. Eleven horses were led into the
gate at the head of the Churchill Downs stretch,

one mile and a quarter from the finish line. The track had dried quickly after a week of sporadic rain, and it was fast. Alydar was the 6–5 favorite with the home crowd, and affirmed was the 9–5 second choice. But now the numbers would give way to the work and the love. Alydar and Affirmed showed that they had received plenty of both. Their chestnut coats were dry, their dispositions relaxed. They were ready. And then they were off.

On the rail inside Affirmed, Raymond Earl was hustled out to the lead by Robert L. Baird, a jockey who was a mere 40 years older than Cauthen. From the far outside, Sensitive Prince rushed toward the front under Mickey Solomone, who was twice Steve's age. In between, the kid went for the position he wanted—third place behind the speed horses, clear of trouble and in striking position.

"There were no surprises for me," said Steve. "Affirmed settled nicely behind Raymond Earl. Then, maybe because he caught sight of Sensitive Prince moving on the outside, he looked outside and drifted a little. Then he settled into stride just the way I wanted him. He knew what was happening."

Cauthen could not know what was happening far behind him. But Velasquez knew all too well. Alydar had only two horses beaten going into the first turn, and the colt did not seem anxious to begin his charge. Echoing a century of Derby jockeys who didn't win, Jorge would speculate later that Alydar just didn't like the feel of the racetrack beneath him.

Up ahead, Solomone was having the opposite problem. Sensitive Prince was too eager, and as he seized the lead from Raymond Earl, he was running much too fast. He surged the first half-mile in 45 3/5 seconds. The fastest half mile ever run by a pacesetter who went on to win a Derby was 45 4/5—by Bold Forbes. And as Solomone and Jerkens were learning more quickly than they had hoped, Sensitive Prince was no Bold Forbes. He managed to put away Raymond Earl, but when the real contenders challenged him on the far turn, Sensitive Prince was finished. Affirmed and Believe It moved to the front as a team. Alydar advanced into fourth place, almost five lengths behind but accelerating. And the lines were drawn.

"I wasn't sure I could put away Believe It," said Steve. "You'd be foolish to ever feel sure about something like that. But I was kind of glad he moved with me. He gave Affirmed something to look at, something to fight for. And that's the way Affirmed runs the best."

Like Cauthen, Eddie Maple had turned in a textbook ride up to the point where he took a narrow lead. Then Maple encountered what has been the final chapter of many good but wasted rides: he ran out of horse. Between the top of the stretch and the eighth pole, Cauthen whipped Affirmed and felt him draw away from the tired Believe It. Then, with the early speed horses destroyed and the hard-trying Believe It dismissed, it was time for the climactic drama that the kid had long anticipated. Waiting for Alydar.

"I hit my horse a few times as he drew away from Believe It," said the kid. "Then I started hand-riding him again, just trying to keep his mind on his business so he could take off again if Alydar came alongside him. And I kept looking back for Alydar."

The majority in the crowd of more than 130,000 were also searching out the favorite. When the devil's-red silks finally flashed into the view of even the infield spectators who spend most of the day watching the backs of other people's necks, a roar filled Churchill Downs. Alydar was making his move at last. But the hopes of his backers faded quickly—at least among those whose vantage points gave them any perspective. The big colt was going to be too late. Just past the sixteenth pole, Alydar swerved inward and bumped Believe It slightly. When he resumed his chase of Affirmed, all hope for him was gone.

.. "By the time I saw Alydar," Steve said with a smile, "I knew I had him beat."

That occasion seemed to call for celebration. Almost a year earlier, when Seattle Slew had completed the Triple Crown sweep by winning the Belmont, jockey Jean Cruguet had raised his whip high above his head just before the finish line. This made a wonderful wire service photo that was circulated all over the world, but it also caused some consternation among racing purists and critics of Cruguet. In hoisting his whip, the jockey had placed himself momentarily off balance in the saddle. Some people had remembered one of the jokes about the rider: "The only way Seattle Slew can get beat is if the Frenchman falls off." And they had pointed out that the Frenchman had dared to court just that possibility.

Such antics never occurred to Cauthen. "Winning a horse race is never an easy thing to do," he said. "When you do it, you can let it speak for itself. The Derby belonged to the Wolfsons and to Laz and a lot of others who worked for it. I didn't have to do anything to show off about it. We beat Alydar. That was enough for people to look at."

The final margin of victory was a length and

a half. Only when it was over, when he had galloped past the finish line and pulled his colt up, did Steve allow himself an unusual gesture. On his way back to the winner's circle, he reached up and doffed his flamingo-pink cap. Unlike Angel Cordero and other flamboyant riders, he was not completely comfortable doing it, and he even looked a bit awkward. And that the perfect finishing touch—a reminder that after the giddy trip from high school in Walton to the winner's circle at the Derby, the kid was still a little shy and innocent. And barely 18.

There were no noticeable tears of joy when it ended. Patrice Jacobs Wolfson had perhaps the best reason for sentiment. Eighteen years earlier, her father had enjoyed what seemed to be his best shot at a Derby, with the great two-year-old Hail to Reason. Hail had also been young Patrice's favorite colt of all. But he had been injured in a workout before he ever got a chance to pursue the classic races. Patrice was keenly aware that she was now savoring that long-awaited Derby victory largely because of a kid who was not yet a year old on the bleak morning when Hail to Reason broke down. But Patrice also had a sense that things eventually work out for those who put their best hopes and efforts into racing. She had inherited that feeling from Hirsch Jacobs and shared it with Lou Wolfson. And so when she hugged the kid in the winner's circle, her eyes were dry and her smile radiant.

Barrera, vindicated in stunning fashion by the victory, had similar instincts. "We raced in California," he said, "and people acted like we had been in China. But I'm a professional and so is Stevie. We knew what this colt could do. Now everybody else knows, too."

In the jockeys' room and again in the press-box news conference, the kid race rider handled the questions with quiet patience and few wry smiles. But he kept the real meaning of the occasion to himself, to be shared in more private moments with Barrera and with Tex and Myra Cauthen. They all knew that the talk of strategy and skillful hand-riding didn't quite capture the experience. In the hard land of Texas and northern Kentucky, in the lean years in Cuba and Mexico, and in the bales of hay in the loft of a Walton barn, they had all learned in their own ways what a Kentucky Derby could really mean. They knew about the hard work and the love of the game. And that special knowledge—and the joy that goes with it—would long outlast the headlines and the quick quotes of the day.

"Do you think he could have run a better race, Steve?" asked somebody who didn't understand.

For a moment the kid looked puzzled. Then the joy flashed in the brown eyes. "What do you want?" Steve Cauthen said softly. "He just won the Kentucky Derby."

ABOUT THE AUTHOR

PETE AXTHELM has been writing a bi-weekly column on
sports and a variety of other subjects as a columnist and
contributing editor for *Newsweek* since 1974. Axthelm
joined the magazine as sports editor in 1968 and still
covers the sports beat extensively, but he has also written
columns and covered stories in the national affairs, international, news media and music sections. Axthelm has
written about thirty *Newsweek* cover stories since he
joined the magazine. His recent covers have ranged over
subjects as diverse as Nadia Comaneci, "Son of Sam"
and Billy Carter. Axthelm's honors include an Eclipse
Award from the Thoroughbred Racing Associations, a pair
of Page One Awards from the New York Newspaper
Guild, a Penney-Missouri Award for journalism about
women, a Silver Gavel Award from the American Bar
Association for reporting in the field of justice, a National
Headliners Award for consistently outstanding columns
and a Schick Award for professional football writing. An
occasional contributor to other magazines such as *Esquire,
Playboy, Classic, New York, Harper's* and *Sport,* Axthelm
is also the author of four books including *The Modern
Confessional Novel,* a work of literary criticism, and *The
City Game,* generally considered the definitive book on
basketball and the inner city. A number of his stories have
also been included in the annual E.P. Dutton anthology,
Best Sports Stories. A native of Rockville Centre, N.Y.,
Axthelm graduated from Yale University in 1965. After
graduation he became the horse racing writer and col-
umist for the *New York Herald Tribune,* and then worked
for *Sports Illustrated* as a staff writer before joining
Newsweek. Axthelm lives in New York City, spends most
of his time on the road in pursuit of columns, and tries to
use his free time profitably at the racetracks of south
Florida, Kentucky and New York.